Inhalt

(Fortsetzung siehe nächste Seite)

... rund um den Satz

Anhang

Lösungen

Autorin: Lindsey Haas
Illustrator: Igor Schulz-Bertram

Vorwort

Liebe Schülerin, lieber Schüler,

geht dir der Englischunterricht manchmal etwas zu schnell? Hast du das Gefühl, wichtiges Grundwissen nicht richtig verstanden zu haben?

Dieses Buch hilft dir, den Stoff der 7. Klasse selbstständig zu trainieren und so deine Englischkenntnisse zu verbessern. Du kannst dich damit gezielt auf **Klassenarbeiten** bzw. **Schulaufgaben** oder die **Nachprüfung** im Fach Englisch vorbereiten.

- Jedes Kapitel beginnt mit **leicht zu verstehenden Erklärungen und Regeln** zur jeweiligen Grammatik, die behandelt wird. Einleuchtende Beispiele verdeutlichen, worauf es in der Praxis ankommt.
- **Vielfältige Aufgaben** – oft ansprechend illustriert und mit landeskundlichem Inhalt – bieten die Möglichkeit, das Erlernte anzuwenden und einzuüben. Besonders schwere Übungen sind mit einem * gekennzeichnet. Bevor du eine Übung bearbeitest, solltest du die Erläuterung zur Aufgabe gründlich durchlesen.
- Im ausführlichen **Lösungsteil** kannst du deine Ergebnisse – natürlich ohne zu mogeln (!) – selbstständig überprüfen. Falls du eine Lösung nicht verstehst oder mit einer Aufgabe einfach nicht zurecht kommst, bitte deine(n) Englischlehrer(in), sie dir zu erklären.

Wenn du mit diesem Buch arbeitest, musst du nicht der Reihe nach vorgehen. Du kannst genau die Bereiche wiederholen, die du noch nicht verstanden hast. Suche einfach im Inhaltsverzeichnis die Kapitel heraus, die für dich wichtig sind. Im betreffenden Kapitel solltest du allerdings alle Übungen zu dem Bereich machen, in dem du dich unsicher fühlst.

Have fun learning my language and I wish you lots of success!

Lindsey Haas

1 Plural – unregelmäßige Pluralformen

Wahrscheinlich ist dir schon lange bekannt, wie man im Englischen Nomen im Singular in den Plural setzt. Es gibt allerdings auch einige Nomen, die **unregelmäßige Pluralformen** haben, und diese muss man nicht nur auswendig lernen, sondern von Zeit zu Zeit auch wiederholen!

Rund um unregelmäßige Pluralformen

Die wichtigsten unregelmäßigen Nomen und ihre Pluralformen

- **Änderung von Vokalen:** Einige Nomen bilden den Plural, indem sie den Vokal verändern.

Beispiele:	man	→	men
	woman	→	women
	child	→	children (das *i* in *children* wird anders ausgeprochen)
	mouse	→	mice
	goose	→	geese
	foot	→	feet
	tooth	→	teeth

- Änderung der **Endung von stimmlos zu stimmhaft:** viele Nomen im Singular, die auf *-f* oder *-fe* enden, bilden ihren Plural, indem man ein *-s* anfügt (dies ist die normale Form der Pluralbildung). Einige Nomen halten sich allerdings nicht an diese Regel. In diesen Ausnahmefällen lautet die Regel wie folgt: die **stimmlose Endung auf *-f*** oder ***-fe*** wird durch das **stimmhafte *-ves* ersetzt**.

Beispiele:	calf → calves		life → lives		thief → thieves	
	half → halves		loaf → loaves		wife → wives	
	knife → knives		self → selves		wolf → wolves	
	leaf → leaves		shelf → shelves			

1. **Making everything plural.** Change the following sentences so that they become plural (nouns, verbs and articles). If there are numbers, change them to *two*; change *a/an* to *some*; change *first person singular* to *first person plural*, etc.

   a) The cat has caught a mouse.
   The cats have caught some mice.

   b) My wife has got a sharp knife in her kitchen.
   ____

   c) A child was playing with a goose.
   ____

   d) The wolf is eating a brown and white calf.
   ____

   e) Is his life interesting?
   ____

   f) One half? No, ______________________________, please.

   g) My tooth hurts.
   ____

   h) The thief stole a loaf of bread.
   ____

   i) That man is very rich.
   ____

   j) I hurt myself this morning.
   __________________________________ this morning.

   k) What tree is that leaf from?
   ____

   l) Has a shelf fallen down?
   ____

- **Wörter auf die Endung *-y*:** Nur solche Nomen, die einen **Vokal vor dem Endungs-*y*** aufweisen, bilden ihre Pluralform auf regelmäßige Weise. In allen anderen Fällen muss das *-y* durch die Endung *-ies* **ersetzt** werden.

Beispiele:	holiday	→	holidays	journey	→	journeys
	donkey	→	donkeys			
	baby	→	babies	country	→	countries
	fly	→	flies			

- **Wörter auf die Endung *-o*:** Einige Nomen, die auf den Vokal *-o* enden, bekommen im Plural die Endung *-es.* Es gibt allerdings auch Nomen, die diese Regel **nicht** einhalten und die **allgemeine Regel** zur Pluralbildung befolgen.

Beispiele:	tomato	→	tomatoes	potato	→	potatoes
	piano	→	pianos	photo	→	photos
	biro	→	biros	kilo	→	kilos

Rund um besondere Fälle

- **Nomen mit einer Form für Singular und Plural:** Einige Wörter wie z.B. *fish, sheep, deer* verändern sich nicht, sie haben im Singular und Plural die **gleiche Form.** Diese musst du dir natürlich einprägen.

  Beispiel: The fish is/are dead.

- ***mass nouns*:** Im Englischen gibt es, anders als im Deutschen, Nomen, die nur eine **Singular-Form** haben. Dies sind die nicht zählbaren oder *mass nouns* wie z.B. *advice, baggage, furniture, infomation, knowledge, news.* Bei der Verwendung dieser Nomen musst du folgendes beachten:

  1. Auf diese Nomen folgen die **Verben immer im Singular.**
  2. Benutze auf keinen Fall den unbestimmten Artikel (*a/an*) mit diesen Nomen, sondern den **bestimmten Artikel (*the*)** oder **einen Begleiter,** z. B. *some.*
  3. Willst du diese Nomen als zählbare Substantive oder Pluralformen verwenden, musst du Wörter wie *a piece of/pieces of* or *a bit of/bits of* verwenden.

Beispiele: That was a good bit of advice you gave me.
General knowledge is very important.
I got some bad news this morning.
Two pieces of my luggage were stolen at the airport.
I heard some interesting bits of information when I was talking to my neighbour.

- **Nomen ohne Singularform:** Es gibt im Englischen einige Nomen (z.B. *police, clothes, pyjamas, jeans, shorts, trousers, scissors, glasses)*, die nur eine Pluralform haben. Auch dieser Sonderfall existiert im Deutschen nicht. Mit diesen Nomen geht immer auch ein **Verb im Plural** einher. Im Englischen geht man davon aus, dass die Gegenstände, die durch diese Nomen bezeichnet werden, aus zwei oder mehr Teilen bestehen. Deshalb haben die Wörter auch keine Form im Singular.

Beispiele: I've lost my glasses. Have you seen them?
In many countries the police are not liked very much.
My trousers are dirty.

2. Translating into English.

a) Die Polizei hat uns keine Informationen gegeben.

____

b) Die Nachrichten, die sie mir gab, waren interessant.

____

c) Gestern konnte ich drei Fische fangen.

____

d) Susannahs neue Brille ist sehr schön.

____

e) Könnten Sie mir einen Rat geben, wo ich billige Möbel kaufen kann?

____

f) Im Sommer gibt es immer viele Fliegen.

____

g) Meine Jeans war teuer.

____

h) Diese Schere ist nicht besonders scharf.

___

i) Ich hätte gerne zwei Kilo Tomaten, bitte.

___

j) Der Bauer hat zwei Esel gekauft. Sie sind sehr laut!

___

k) Meine Kleider sind etwas dreckig.

___

l) Der Müll riecht furchtbar.

___

m) Die Schafe in den Bergen haben ein schweres Leben.

___

n) Die Bilder von deinem Urlaub sind gut.

___

2 Unbestimmte Pronomen und Begleiter: *some* und *any*

Some und ***any*** können als unbestimmte Pronomen und Begleiter auftreten. Als **Pronomen** werden sie anstelle eines Nomens verwendet, als **Begleiter** sind sie Teil einer Nominalphrase. Als Begleiter haben *some* und *any* weitestgehend die gleiche Bedeutung wie der unbestimmte Artikel *a/an.* Sie bezeichnen eine Menge ohne genaue Angaben zu machen. Im Gegensatz zu *a/an* verwendest du sie aber nur bei **nicht zählbaren Nomen** *(uncountable nouns)* und **Nomen, die im Plural** *(plural nouns)* stehen.

Beispiele: I haven't got a bicycle. (singular countable noun)
They haven't got any bananas in that shop. (plural noun)
I need some help. (uncountable noun)

Rund um *some* und *any*

Wie benutzt du *some* und *any*?

- Als allgemeine Regel kannst du dir merken, dass *some* nur in **bejahten Aussagesätzen** benutzt wird.

  Beispiel: I'd like to buy some football boots, please. Size 41.

- *any* benutzt du, wenn du eine **Frage** stellst oder einen **verneinten Satz** bildest.

  Beispiel: Have you got any bananas?
  No, sorry, I haven't got any bananas.

- Wenn du eine **Frage** stellst und davon ausgehst, dass die **Antwort „yes“** sein wird, oder du jemanden zur Antwort „yes“ ermutigen möchtest (wenn du z.B. jemandem etwas anbieten möchtest), dann musst du *some* und **nicht** *any* benutzen.

  Beispiele: (At the fruit shop): “Could I have <u>some</u> apples, please?”
  (Im Normalfall hat der Obsthändler immer Äpfel.)

  Would you like <u>some</u> more ice-cream?
  (Die Frage mit *any* zu stellen, wäre sehr unhöflich.)

- Wenn du davon **ausgehst,** dass die **Antwort wahrscheinlich nicht „yes“** sein wird, musst du *any* verwenden.

  Beispiel: Have you got <u>any</u> strawberries left?
  (Die Erdbeersaison ist fast vorbei und du denkst, dass wahrscheinlich keine mehr übrig sind. Trotzdem hoffst du, dass es welche gibt.)

- Triffst du auf einen bejahten Aussagesatz, der **Negationen** (Verneinungswörter) enthält, wie z. B. *never, without, hardly*, dann ändert sich die Bedeutung und der Satz bekommt einen negativen Charakter. In solchen Fällen musst du *any* und nicht *some* benutzen.

  Beispiele: You <u>never</u> give me <u>any</u> help with my homework.
  There are <u>hardly</u> <u>any</u> sweets left in the box.
  We found the way <u>without</u> <u>any</u> trouble at all.

- In **Bedingungssätzen** *(conditional sentences)* mit *if* kannst du entweder *some* oder *any* benutzen, ohne eine Bedeutungsänderung herbeizuführen.

  Beispiel: If you want <u>some</u>/<u>any</u> more money, just let me know and I’ll give it to you.

- Du kannst *some* und *any* auch alleine **ohne Nomen** benutzen. Sie **ersetzen** dann das Nomen und werden als **Pronomen**, nicht als Begleiter eingesetzt.

  Beispiele: Would you like <u>any</u> more <u>coffee</u>?
  No thanks, I’ve still got <u>some</u>.

  Did you get the <u>newspaper</u>?
  No, they hadn’t got <u>any</u>.

1. Decisions. Decide whether you need *some* or *any* to complete these sentences.

a) 

Have you got ____________ sausages?

≈ Sorry, not today but I have got ____________ frankfurters. They're very good. Would you like to try ______________ ?

b) 

Have you possibly got _____________ stamps? I need to send a postcard to my friend before I go home.

≈ No, sorry, I haven't got ________ but they've got __________ at the post office next door.

c) 

I'd like ________________ aspirin, please.

d) 

There's hardly _______________ tea in the pot. Can you make ______________ more, please, Andrew?

e) 

If you want ______________________ more ice-cream, Polly, you'll have to get it yourself. It's in the freezer.

Rund um Zusammensetzungen mit *some* und *any*

Für die Verwendung der Zusammensetzungen *someone/anyone, somebody/anybody, something/anything, somewhere/anywhere* gelten die gleichen Regeln wie für die Wörter, aus denen sie hervorgehen. *Any* oder eine Zusammensetzung mit *any* kann allerdings auch im bejahten Aussagesatz auftreten. Es hat dann eine **Sonderbedeutung.**

- *any* (und alle seine Zusammensetzungen) kann auch bedeuten: ‚it doesn't matter which/who/what/where/when'.

  Beispiele: You can catch any train: they all go to Waterloo Station.
  (Du kannst jeden Zug nehmen.)

  Just come any time. I'm always at home in the afternoons.
  (Komm einfach irgendwann.)

  Anywhere is OK. I just don't want to stay at home all summer.
  (Jeder Ort ist okay. /Es ist mir egal, wohin.)

  Anybody could have stolen the picture. We just don't know.
  (Jeder hätte das Bild stehlen können.)

  You can choose anything you want from the menu.
  (Du kannst dir von der Karte bestellen, was immer du willst.)

- In allen anderen (allgemeinen) bejahten Aussagesätzen müssen jedoch die bekannten Grundregeln eingehalten werden: Benutze immer *some* und nicht *any*. Die Bedeutung von ***some + compound*** (Zusammensetzung) ist dann „irgend + ... (einer/wer/wann usw.)".

  Beispiele: Somebody will help you. (Irgendjemand wird dir helfen.)
  Something's going to happen soon. (Irgendetwas wird passieren.)
  I've seen that man somewhere before.
  (Ich habe diesen Mann schon irgendwo gesehen.)

2. Croeso i Gymru. Using *some*, *any* and their compounds (*something, anybody*, etc.) complete this short description of the smallest country in Great Britain.

Do you know ______________________ about Wales? Well, let me tell you ________________ about this small country. Because Wales belongs to the United Kingdom, ________________ from England, Scotland or Northern Ireland can cross the border into Wales without a passport. But once ________________ is in Wales, they will see that the geography, traditions, culture and language are very different. Welsh is not spoken all over Wales. In fact hardly ________________ speaks it in the southern and eastern parts but if you ask ________________________ in north or west Wales if they can speak Welsh, you will have a 50 % chance of them saying "yes".

Snowdonia National Park

The southern and eastern parts of the country are industrial. ___________ you go in the valleys, you will find mining villages although quite a lot have been closed. However, _______________ have been opened to the public so people can see what a miner's life is like.
Although small, some very famous people have come from Wales. _________________ in Britain will be able to tell you that the poet Dylan Thomas was Welsh, that the actors Richard Burton and Anthony Hopkins are Welsh too and that the country produced __________________ well-known politicians: David Lloyd-George (Prime Minister 1916–1918), Aneurin Bevan (Labour MP during and after Winston Churchill), Michael Foot and Neil Kinnock (both heads of the Labour Party when Margaret Thatcher was Conservative Prime Minister).
Because there's hardly ________________ industry in north-west Wales, the countryside is still beautiful. Here you will find Snowdonia National Park and the famous mountain Mount Snowdon which is 1,085 m high.

3 Das Stützwort *one*

Das sogenannte Stützwort *one* (Plural: *ones)* hat vor allem eine **stilistische Funktion** im Satz. Du kannst einen Satz auch derart formulieren, dass *one/ones* überflüssig werden. Werden sie aber eingesetzt, bekommen die jeweiligen Sätze eine bessere stilistische Qualität, d.h. sie klingen besser oder drücken einen Umstand noch trefflicher aus. Vergleiche die folgenden Satzpaare:

Beispiele: I want to buy a new bicycle. I'd really like a red bicycle.
I want to buy a new bicycle. I'd really like a red one.

Which apples do you want?
The red apples, please.
The red ones, please.

Du merkst sofort, dass jeweils der zweite Satz in diesen Beispielen besser klingt und natürlicher wirkt. Mit *one/ones* kannst du also **ein Nomen ersetzen,** das du vorher schon einmal verwendet hast. Diese beiden kleinen Stützwörter ermöglichen es dir, das vorher benutzte Nomen nicht noch einmal wiederholen zu müssen. Mit ihrer Hilfe werden deine Sätze besser klingen und du kannst dich auf das Nötigste beschränken.

Rund um das Stützwort *one/ones*

Wann benutzt du *one*, wann *ones*?

- Mit *one* kannst du zählbare Nomen im **Singular** ersetzen.

  Beispiel: My little sister got a rabbit for her birthday. It's a black one.

- Mit *ones* kannst du zählbare Nomen im **Plural** ersetzen.

  Beispiel: Those black shoes are much nicer than the blue ones.

1. The Beatles. Billy has prepared a paper about the *Beatles*. He has learnt it by heart and has only noted down the most important adjectives to help him remember the sentences. Can you find out which adjective goes with which sentence? Use *one* or *ones* together with a suitable adjective from the list to complete the sentences. Use each adjective *once only*.

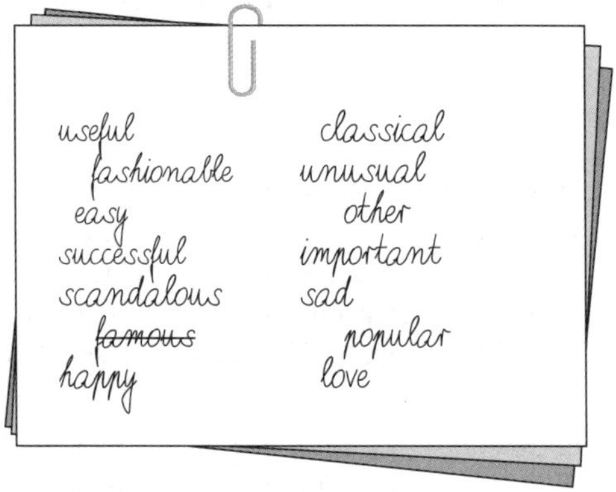

a) Until Wednesday, 24 October 1962 *The Beatles* were an unknown group from Liverpool but today it is the most _famous_ _one_ in the world. On that date they shot to Number 27 in the British Top Thirty charts.

b) *Love me Do* was the title of the hit which first made them famous back in 1962 but since then they have had many ________________ ________

c) Although the group quickly became popular, the road to success was not an ________________ ________.

d) John Lennon and Paul McCartney spent many afternoons listening to the songs of American stars such as Chuck Berry and Elvis Presley before they could write the ______________________ Lennon and McCartney ________ which everyone knows even today.

e) In the early years they played in night-clubs in Liverpool and Hamburg. This experience was a ________________ ________ because it helped them later when they had to play to big audiences.

f) Everything about *The Beatles* was new and exciting, not just their music. Their hairstyle was very different and it became a very ______________ ____________________.

g) Many people influenced the careers of George Harrison, John Lennon, Paul McCartney and Ringo Starr but the most ____________________ ________ were Brian Epstein and George Martin.

h) The four boys did not just play traditional instruments but also ________________ _________ as well such as combs.

i) If you listen to their songs, you can hear that many different styles of music influenced the lads from Liverpool: they mixed ________________ and ________________ _________ together to make a new and original sound.

j) Just like Princess Diana in the 80s and 90s, *The Beatles*, in the 1960s, were always in the news headlines – for many different reasons – including ________________ _________ .

k) For example, some people say that there are hidden messages about drugs in their songs (e. g. Lucy in the Sky with Diamonds). Even so, no-one can take away the fact that John, Paul, George and Ringo wrote and sang songs which people today still sing. Some were ____________ _________, others were ________________ _________ and very often they were ________________ _________. It doesn't matter. There was, and still is, something there for everybody.

Wie bildest du Konstruktionen mit *one/ones?*

- Taucht vor *one(s)* ein **Adjektiv** auf, musst du einen **Artikel** benutzen. Hier kannst du sowohl den unbestimmten (*a/an*) als auch den bestimmten (*the*) Artikel benutzen.

Beispiele:

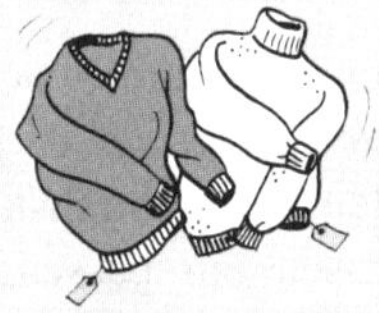

Can I have the red one, please?

I'd like a new one for my birthday.

- Steht vor *one(s)* **kein Adjektiv**, kannst du den **unbestimmten Artikel nicht** benutzen.

Beispiel:

Can I have a small one without cream, please?

Can I have one without cream, please?

- Wenn du dich auf ein bestimmtes Objekt beziehst und es steht vor *one(s)* kein Adjektiv, musst du den **bestimmten Artikel** setzen.

Beispiel:

I prefer the black one with the red buttons.

I prefer the one with the pockets.

Wie werden *one/ones* übersetzt?

- Man kann *one/ones* nicht direkt ins Deutsche übersetzen. Im Deutschen lässt du oft einfach das Nomen, das wiederholt werden müsste, weg und verwendest stattdessen das begleitende Adjektiv als Nomen.

Beispiel: Kann ich *das rote* haben, bitte?

(*rot* wird hier anstelle von *Fahrrad* verwendet.)

Can I have *the red one*, please?

(*one* wird anstelle von *bicycle* verwendet.)

- Nicht alle Adjektive, die im Deutschen als Nomen verwendet werden können, können im Englischen auch durch *one(s)* wiedergegeben werden. Wenn du über **Menschen** (oder auch Haustiere) sprichst, darfst du *one(s)* nicht benutzen, sondern musst stattdessen ein passendes Nomen verwenden, wie z. B. *person, man, child.*

Beispiel: Am Wochenende schläft die Kleine bei uns, weil ihre Eltern ins Kino gehen.

The little girl /My granddaughter is sleeping at our house at the weekend because her parents are going to the cinema.

2. Shopping list. You are staying with an English family. Your friend's mother has given you a shopping list and asked you both to go shopping for her. But, she hasn't told you which **sort** of things to buy. Complete the dialogue, using the shopping list and the words next to it to help you.

French	Swiss
fruit	natural
red	green
Indian	Chinese
chocolate	plain
brown	white
cheap	expensive

a) Which cheese should we buy – the French one or the Swiss one?
≈ I think we should get the Swiss one.

b) Which yoghurts should we buy – ______ or ______?
≈ I'd prefer ______.

c) Which apples shall we get – ______ or ______?
≈ Let's get ______.

d) Which tea do you want to get – ______ or ______?
≈ Why don't we get ______?

e) Which biscuits do you prefer – ______ or ______?
≈ I like ______ more.

f) Which eggs should we get – ________________ or ________________?
≈ We usually get ____.

g) Which toothpaste do you want – ____________ or ________________?
≈ I don't think we should buy ________________________________.

3. Cambridge. Read the following text and then complete it, using the indefinite, definite or no article as necessary.

Have you ever heard of the town of Cambridge? It's ______________ one which is famous for its old university, just like Oxford too. When the university started in the 13th century, it was small. Today it has over 20 colleges: ____________ oldest one is Peterhouse (1284) and ____________ youngest one is Robinson College which was opened in 1977. ___________ particularly famous one is King's College, because of its beautiful chapel. King's College also has a choir, ______________ one which is well known all over the world.

Until 1871 no women could go to Cambridge University because there were no women's colleges and until the 1970s men and women were taught separately: women went to the 3 women's colleges and men went to ____________ other ones. Although the colleges are today nearly all mixed, there are still more male students than ______________ female ones.

4. Translating. How would you translate these sentences into English without using *one(s)*? Find a suitable noun to go with the adjective which you have already got.

a) Es gefällt mir nicht, wie die Katze aussieht. Die Arme muss zum Tierarzt.

____

____

____

b) Das einzig komplizierte an diesem Spiel ist der Anfang.

____

____

c) Die Polizei hat einen sehr schwierigen Fall *(case)* zu lösen: Sie haben einen unbekannten Toten gefunden.

____

____

____

d) Tina hat eine enge Beziehung *(relationship)* zu ihren Großeltern. Die Kleine verbringt jedes Wochenende dort.

____

____

____

____

e) Keine wusste, wer der Arme war.

____

f) Die Neue in unserer Klasse kommt aus Berlin.

____

g) Das Interessante ist, dass keiner sah, wer den Stein warf.

____

____

Was musst du noch über *one(s)* wissen?

- *one(s)* kann nur **zählbare** Nomen wie z. B. *bottle, bicycle, book, girl, comb, apple* ersetzen.

  Beispiel: If you see a metal comb, could you get me one, please?

- **Nicht zählbare Nomen** wie z. B. *happiness, energy, water, flour, oil* können nicht durch *one(s)* ersetzt werden. Hier musst du normalerweise das Nomen wiederholen.

  Beispiel: I don't like swimming in dirty water.
  The water in the lake near my house is very clean.

- Nach einem **Superlativ** kannst du *one(s)* auch weglassen.

  Beispiel: My dog is the nicest (one) in the world.

- Nach **Demonstrativpronomen** wie *this/that, these/those* kannst du *one(s)* weglassen, wenn **kein Adjektiv** dabei ist.

  Beispiele: I'm going to buy this (one), not that (one).
  I'm going to buy this green one, not that blue one.

- Nach ***both*** musst du *one(s)* normalerweise weglassen.

  Beispiel: Bob: Would you like the black one or the white one?
  Mary: Both, please.

- Nach **Zahlen** musst du *one(s)* weglassen, wenn **kein Adjektiv** dabei steht.

  Beispiel: Tom: How many fish did you catch?
  Steve: I caught three. I caught three big ones.

✷ **5. Places in London.** Complete these sentences using *(the) one(s)* where possible to replace another word and try not to repeat yourself. Sometimes you won't be able to replace the word and sometimes you will be able to leave *(the) one(s)* out! Take care.

a) If you listen to the BBC radio news, you will hear the sound of the bells of *Big Ben* ring out every hour. *Big Ben* is inside the clock tower which is next to the Houses of Parliament. In fact there are five bells inside this tower and ____________________ which is the largest is *Big Ben*.

b) In and around London there are ten royal parks but _________ closest ____________ to Buckingham Palace, the official home of the Queen and her family, is St. James's Park.

c) Like all big cities, London has got many different kinds of museums. ____________________ which many children like the best are *Madame Tussaud's Wax Museum* in Baker Street and *The Science Museum* in Knightsbridge.

d) Do you know which of these 'churches' is more important to the Royal Family: St. Paul's Cathedral or Westminster Abbey?
≈ Both ___________ are although more royal events have taken place in Westminster Abbey – kings and queens have been crowned and buried there for many centuries and the Queen was also married there.

e) There are many famous streets in London. There are those ___________ which are famous for shopping such as Knightsbridge, Oxford Street or The Kings Road or those _______________ which tourists go to to buy souvenirs such as Carnaby Street or Portobello Road. And of course there are those _____________________ which people have heard of for business reasons such as Fleet Street (newspapers) or Threadneedle Street (banks). One street we've not talked about is Downing Street, __________________ in which the Prime Minister lives, at Number Ten, and the Chancellor of the Exchequer, at Number Eleven.

f) The Tower of London was built by William the Conqueror in around 1079. This famous building has been used for several different purposes but ______________ is hardly known by anybody: London Zoo, before it moved to Regents Park, was in the moat of the Tower!

g) London is divided up into political parts called 'boroughs'. There are eleven ______________ around the City and 20 outer ______________. ______________ which are around the City are called inner boroughs.

Rund um Fragen mit *which one ...?/which ones ...?*

- Wenn du eine Frage stellen möchtest und dabei die Antwortmöglichkeiten auf einige wenige reduzieren möchtest, dann kannst du *which (one) ...?* benutzen, wenn du dich auf einen einzelnen Gegenstand **(Singular)** beziehst; *which (ones) ...?* benutzt du dann, wenn du dich auf mehrere Gegenstände beziehst **(Plural)** oder zumindest auf Nomen, die im Englischen Pluralformen haben, wie z. B. *jeans, trousers, glasses, scissors.*

Beispiele: Which {(one) / (bike)} would you like: red, green, black or gold?

Which {(ones) / (gloves)} would you like: the expensive ones or the cheap ones?

Which {(ones) / (sunglasses)} would you like: these for £2.50 or those for £3.29?

Sobald du die Frageform mit *which one(s) ...?* wählst, kann der Antwortgeber nur noch eine bestimmte Anzahl von Antworten geben.

- Wenn Fragesteller und Antwortgeber beide wissen, um was es geht, dann kannst du das Nomen beruhigt weglassen. Wenn du jedoch über ein neues Thema sprichst, dann musst du das Nomen nach *which* unbedingt nennen.

Beispiele: Mary: I've got three new jumpers.
Bob: Which do you like best? (es ist klar, um was es geht)
Tina: Which book do you like best, *Momo* or *Pippi Longstocking?* (ein neues Thema wird eingeführt)

6. Shopping with a friend. Look at the different pictures and then write short dialogues using *which ...?* Make sure you answer correctly too! If no answer is given, choose yourself.

a) 

Dad: Which cat do you want, Tara? The grey or the black one?

Tara: The black one, please, Daddy.

b) 

Mum: ________ ____________ do you want, Sam? The racing bike or the mountain bike?

Sam: ____________________, please, Mum.

c) 

Tom: ________ ______________ are you going to buy, Ann: _________ ____________ or __________?

Ann: ______________________________ because I've only got £50.

d) 

Tina: _______ _____________ do you prefer, Kathy? This __________?

Kathy: No, I ________________________.

e) 

Tom: _______ ________ are you going to send to Mum and Dad, Sandra: The River Thames, Buckingham Palace or The Royal Family?

Sandra: I think I'll __________________.

4 Wie Wörter gebildet werden: Wortfamilien

Die englische Sprache besteht nicht nur aus Grammatik, sondern auch aus Wörtern, aus Vokabular. Das Vokabular einer Sprache muss **regelmäßig** gelernt werden, am besten alle zwei Tage einmal. Du wirst bald Fortschritte erkennen, wenn du deine Wörter statt einmal pro Woche 30 Minuten, 3 mal die Woche je 10 Minuten wiederholst.

Beim Nachschauen eines neuen Wortes in deinem Wörterbuch wirst du oft merken, dass dieses Wort zu einer **Wortfamilie** gehört: Der Stamm dieses Wortes ist auch in etlichen anderen Wörtern zu finden. Das Ende des Wortes ändert sich je nach der **Funktion** des Wortes im Satz.

Beispiele: Why does it always rain on my birthday? (Verb)
It's been a very rainy day. (Adjektiv)
The rain won't stop. (Nomen)

Auf diese Weise kannst du dir nicht nur ein Wort, sondern gleich zwei oder drei neue Wörter, vielleicht sogar eine ganze neue Wortfamilie aneignen!

Mit einem **Karteikasten** und kleinen **Karteikärtchen** kannst du dir die Arbeit mit dem englischen Wortschatz erleichtern: Auf einer Seite schreibst du jedes neue Wort (oder besser noch seine Familie) auf **Englisch**, auf der anderen Seite die jeweilige Entsprechung auf **Deutsch**.

rain (noun) to rain (verb) rainy (adjective)	Regen (Nomen) regnen (Verb) regnerisch (Adjektiv)

Mit diesen Kärtchen kannst du die Reihenfolge der Vokabeln beliebig verändern und dich besser selbst testen als mit einer starren Vokabelliste aus dem Buch oder aus dem Vokabelheft.

Rund um die Wortbildung: Nomen → Adjektiv

Bestimmte Nomen bilden ihre entsprechenden Adjektive immer auf die gleiche Weise: Eine der größten Gruppen dieser Art sind alle **Wörter rund ums Wetter.**

- Man bildet das Adjektiv, indem man an das Nomen ein *-y* anfügt.

  Beispiel: rain → rainy

- Bei einsilbigen Nomen mit Vokal vor dem letzten Konsonanten musst du diesen verdoppeln, bevor das *-y* angehängt wird.

  Beispiel: fog → foggy

1. Matching. Match the noun to the correct picture.

a) rain

b) snow

c) cloud

d) fog

e) sun

2. Weather report. Read the following weather report. Underline all the weather nouns you find and put a circle around all the weather adjectives.

"Good evening, this is Lana Roberts with the weather report until tomorrow evening. There's heavy fog in the Norfolk area and there will be no change until midday tomorrow. Here in London it's cool and cloudy. No rain is expected until tomorrow night. Up in rainy Scotland it doesn't seem the weather is ever going to change. I'm afraid it's not a good day for going outside. Out on the south-west coast it's warm and sunny. The sun just won't stop shining. In the north-east of England the windy conditions are causing big problems at sea. The wind is expected to become less strong by tomorrow morning. The clouds over the Midlands will disappear by midday. Tomorrow afternoon will be warm with perhaps a little rain in the evening. Now briefly over to Europe. In southern Germany the weather is perfect for skiing: lots of snow but also sunny. We expect these snowy conditions to continue all this week. That's all for today. Good night."

3. Weather symbols. Using the text from the weather report in exercise 2 and the symbols shown at the side, mark the weather on the map.

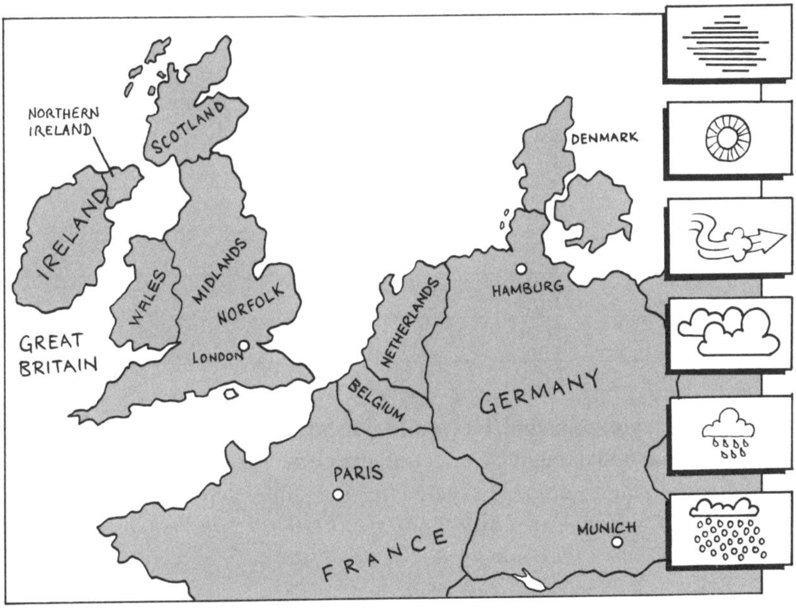

- Es gibt noch **weitere Nomen** (einige davon haben nichts mit dem Wetter zu tun), die ihre Adjektive auf die gleiche Weise bilden wie diejenigen, die wir schon kennengelernt haben.

  Beispiel: dirt → dirty

- Ausnahme bei der **Schreibung:** Wenn das Substantiv auf *-e* endet, entfällt dieses beim Adjektiv, bzw. wird zu *-y.*

  Beispiel: ice → icy

4. Vocabulary expansion (English). Complete the **white sections only** of this table with the correct form of the English noun or adjective. Take care with the spelling!

noun	**translation**	**adjective**	**translation**
storm	Sturm	stormy	stürmisch
		smelly	
noise			
		funny	
hunger			
		juicy	
		thirsty	
sun			
rock			
salt			
		sandy	

5. Vocabulary expansion (German translation). Complete the **grey sections only** of the above table by selecting the correct translation: *hungrig – ~~Sturm~~ – durstig – Salz – saftig – sandig – felsig – Saft – sonnig – Spaß – stinkend – ~~stürmisch~~ – Hunger – Lärm – Durst – Felsen – Sand – Gestank /Geruch – salzig – Sonne – laut – lustig/komisch/seltsam.*

6. Word making. Look at the pictures. Then find a noun and an adjective which describe them correctly. Write them in the space provided.

a) 

noisy neighbours

b) 

c) 

d) 

Rund um die Wortbildung: Verb → Adjektiv

- Im Englischen gibt es mehrere **Nachsilben**, mit deren Hilfe man aus Verben Adjektive bilden kann. Eine sehr gebräuchliche Nachsilbe ist ***-able.*** *-able* bedeutet „es kann ... werden".

  Beispiel: The book I got for my birthday is very enjoyable.
  = The book I got for my birthday can be enjoyed very much.

- Einige **Verben auf *-e*** verlieren dieses, bevor die Nachsilbe *-able* angehängt wird.

  Beispiel: to believe → believable

- Adjektive, die **vor** dem letzten Konsonanten einen **betonten Vokal** haben, **verdoppeln** diesen.

  Beispiel: to forget → forgettable

- Um ein Adjektiv ins **Gegenteil** zu verkehren, musst du die **Vorsilbe *un-*** vor das bereits aus dem Verb gebildete Adjektiv stellen. Einige Adjektive können allerdings nicht auf diese Weise ihr Gegenteil bilden. In diesem Fall musst du ein anderes passendes Adjektiv finden.

  Beispiele: My teacher told me he couldn't correct my homework because it was unreadable.
  = ... because it could not be read.

	verb	***adjective***	***prefix + adjective***
	to believe	believable	unbelievable
	to read	readable	unreadable
	to break	breakable	unbreakable
	to wash	washable	unwashable
Ausnahme:	to understand	understandable	— (or: incomprehensible)

7. Formation practice. Complete this table by filling in the gaps.

verb	translation	adjective	translation	prefix + adjective
to agree	*zustimmen*	agreeable	*angenehm*	unagreeable disagreeable
to break	*(zer)brechen*		*zerbrechlich*	
to change	*ändern*		*veränderlich*	
to forget	*vergessen*		*(leicht zu) vergessen*	
to imagine	*sich etw. einbilden, vorstellen*		*vorstellbar*	
to like	*mögen*		*nett*	
to love	*lieben*		*liebenswert*	
to reason	*begründen*		*vernünftig*	
to sink	*versinken*		*versinkbar*	
to think	*denken*		*denkbar*	

8. Crossword – missing adjectives. Using the clues to help you, complete the crossword.

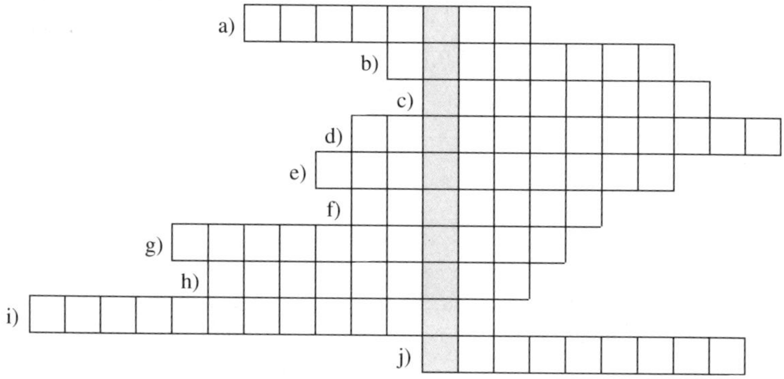

a) These clothes are only hand ________________.

b) I can't put this book down: it's so ________________.

c) Maria is a very ________________ girl. Everyone thinks she is nice.

d) An ________________ thing has happened. I got a 1– in my English test! It's amazing.

e) These prices are ________________ (beat). Nowhere else is cheaper.

f) All small animals and babies are ________________. Perhaps it is because they are so helpless.

g) It's ______________________ (think): Tim told the teacher he thinks homework is a waste of time.

h) Don't worry. The plates are made of plastic: they are not ___________.

i) I will always remember our holiday in South Africa last year. It was ________________. I often think about it.

j) Did you have an ________________ (enjoy) weekend? ≈ No, it was terrible.

The hidden word is: ________________.

Rund um die Wortbildung: Verb → Nomen

- Es gibt im Englischen viele Verben, die als Stamm dienen für Nomen, die **Leute und ihre Tätigkeiten** (Jobs, Hobbys) beschreiben. Um diese Nomen zu bilden, musst du die Endung *-er* an das jeweilige Verb anhängen.

  Beispiele: to paint → painter
  to climb → climber

- Endet das Verb auf ***-e***, musst du nur noch ein *-r* an den Stamm anfügen.

  Beispiel: to ride → rider

- Bei **einsilbigen** Verben mit einen **Vokal vor** dem letzten Konsonanten, wird der Konsonant **verdoppelt,** bevor *-er* an den Stamm angehängt wird.

  Beispiel: to win → winner

- Aber pass auf: Es gibt zusätzliche **Ausnahmen!**

  Beispiele: to travel → traveller
  to visit → visitor

9. Guess what this person does. Complete the following table.

a)	This person	rides horses.	He's a / She's a	rider.
b)		listens to the radio.		
c)		travels a lot.		
d)		sings all day.		
e)		interviews pop stars and famous people.		
f)		is always dreaming.		
g)		has lost a lot of money gambling.		
h)		likes climbing mountains.		
i)		swims in races.		
j)		builds houses.		

Bei der Bildung einiger Nomen wird zur Verdeutlichung der Bedeutung nicht nur der Verbstamm benötigt, sondern eine Verbindung von Nomen und Verb. Erst an diese Verbindung hängst du dann die *-er* Endung an.

Beispiel: A landowner is someone who owns land.

10. Explaining jobs. Write explanations for what these people do.

a watchmaker ________________________

a newsreader ________________________

a storyteller ________________________

a weight lifter ________________________

11. Look at the pictures and then guess what job the person has.

a) 

reporter

b) 

____

c) 

____

d)  ____________________

e) 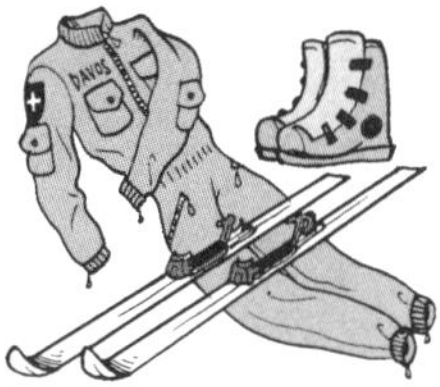 ____________________

12. What do they need? Choose *one* of the pictures for each of the people in exercise 11 and write a sentence using words from the noun and verb families you know.

a) A reporter needs a tape recorder to report.

b) ____________________

c) ____________________

d) ____________________

e) ____________________

13. Putting it all together. Look at the letters below. Find the words (nouns/adjectives/verbs which you have studied in this chapter) and put a circle around them. They are written horizontally (← →) and vertically (↓↑). There are **22** words to find. The first one has already been done for you. Good luck!

b	e	z	f	a	c	u	n	r	e	a	d	a	b	l	e
r	i	p	l	o	s	m	e	l	l	y	i	e	e	i	s
e	i	w	u	s	i	n	g	e	r	m	r	o	o	s	u
a	n	p	a	i	n	t	g	a	f	l	t	a	s	t	n
k	t	h	i	n	k	s	r	j	o	p	r	i	d	e	n
a	e	d	f	s	a	h	i	u	r	t	h	r	o	n	y
b	r	e	a	d	l	f	n	i	g	w	i	n	n	e	r
l	v	i	s	i	t	o	r	c	e	i	m	o	n	r	g
e	i	n	h	a	t	g	s	y	t	n	o	i	t	i	o
f	e	t	s	o	s	i	l	o	l	d	p	s	a	l	t
s	w	i	m	m	e	r	b	i	c	y	d	e	o	l	t
c	e	u	n	d	e	r	s	t	a	n	d	a	b	l	e
y	r	a	i	n	y	a	b	l	m	a	t	z	e	r	l

5 Adjektive

Adjektive sind Wörter wie *old, difficult, red,* die Nomen begleiten oder auch nach bestimmten Verben stehen und uns Einzelheiten über sie verraten bzw. uns mit den verschiedensten Informationen über sie versorgen.

Beispiele: My mother bought me a red bike.
My bike is old.

5.1 Steigerung und Vergleiche

Du steigerst Adjektive, wenn du verschiedene **Abstufungen von Eigenschaften** ausdrücken willst. Es gibt zwei Steigerungsformen, den **Komparativ** *(comparative)* und den **Superlativ** *(superlative)*. Du kannst mit den Steigerungsformen auch **Vergleiche** bilden.

Beispiele: My bike is older. (1. Steigerungsform = Komparativ)
Exercise one is the most difficult and exercise four is the least difficult. (2. Steigerungsform = Superlativ)
My bike is older than Susan's bike. (Vergleich)

Rund um die Steigerung von Adjektiven

Wie bildest du den Komparativ und den Superlativ?

- Bei den meisten **einsilbigen Adjektiven** und **zweisilbigen Adjektiven** auf ***-ow*, *-er*** und ***-le*** musst du bei der Steigerung *-er* oder *-est* an die Grundform anhängen.

	Grundform	Komparativ	Superlativ
Beispiele:	short	shorter	(the) shortest
	clever	cleverer	(the) cleverest

- Bei Adjektiven mit einem **kurzen einfachen Vokal**, auf den ein Konsonant folgt, musst du den Endkonsonanten verdoppeln und *-er* oder *-est* anhängen.

Beispiel:	fat	fatter	(the) fattest

- Wenn das **Adjektiv auf *-e*** endet, musst du einfach *-r* oder *-st* anfügen.

Beispiel:	late	later	(the) latest

- Endet ein **zweisilbiges Adjektiv auf *-y***, dann ändere das *-y* zu *i* und füge einfach die normalen Steigerungsformen an.

Beispiel:	happy	happier	(the) happiest

- Einige Adjektive haben **unregelmäßige Steigerungsformen**. Diese musst du auswendig lernen.

Beispiele:	good	better	(the) best
	bad	worse	(the) worst
	little	less	(the) least
	much/many	more	(the) most
	far	further	(the) furthest
		farther	(the) farthest

1. What's missing? Complete the table.

small	*smaller*	the smallest
hot		
	further	
		the busiest
white		
sweet		
clever		
	friendlier	
		the oldest
	worse	

- Bei **zweisilbigen Adjektiven,** die **nicht auf *-le, -y, -er* und *-ow* enden,** und bei **Adjektiven mit drei oder mehr Silben,** musst du *more* bzw. *most* (oder *less/least)* vor die Grundform des Adjektivs setzen.

  Beispiele: boring — more boring — (the) most boring
  exciting — less exciting — (the) least exciting

- Eine Ausnahme ist das Adjektiv *fun:*

  Beispiel: fun — more fun — (the) most fun

2. Opposites. Find the opposites of these comparatives or superlatives. You must use another word!

a) hotter – *colder*

b) more difficult – ______________________

c) cheaper – ______________________

d) the furthest – ______________________

e) younger – ______________________

f) the most boring – ______________________
g) worse – ______________________
h) more – ______________________
i) the most stupid – ______________________
j) prettier – ______________________
k) heaviest – ______________________

3. Making comparisons. Look at the pictures and then complete the sentences using the comparative or superlative forms of the adjectives.

a) 

Susan's motor bike is ______________. (big)

b) 

The weather is a bit ______________ today. (good)

c) 

Which animal is ________________? (fast)

d) 

Mum: Why can't you be ______________, Nicola? (careful)

e) 

Which is __________, a tortoise or a snail? (slow)

Rund um den Vergleich

Mit den Steigerungsformen kannst du auch einen **Vergleich** zwischen zwei oder mehreren Dingen, Personen usw. bilden. Dieser Vergleich kann **Gleichheit** oder **Ungleichheit** ausdrücken.

Wie bildest du die Vergleichsformen des Komparativs?

- Bei **dem Vergleich von zwei unterschiedlichen Dingen** benötigst du die Komparativform des Adjektivs + *than.*

  Beispiele: London is <u>bigger</u> <u>than</u> Manchester.
  A motorbike is <u>more dangerous</u> <u>than</u> a car.

- Wenn du **die Gleichheit zweier Dinge** ausdrücken willst, benötigst du *as* + Grundform des Adjektivs + *as.*

  Beispiele: My friend is <u>as</u> <u>old</u> <u>as</u> me.
  These jeans are <u>as</u> <u>expensive</u> <u>as</u> those ones.

- Wenn du die **Ungleichheit zweier Dinge** ausdrücken willst, kannst du es entweder so wie oben mit *than* tun oder mit *not* + *as* + Grundform des Adjektivs + *as*.

  Beispiele: Manchester is not as big as London.
  A car is not as dangerous as a motorbike.

Warum gibt es mehrere Möglichkeiten das Gleiche auszudrücken?

Ganz einfach: Wenn du schreibst, willst du nicht, dass jeder Satz gleich anfängt oder den gleichen Stil hat. Was du schreibst, soll sich ja interessant anhören. Also brauchst du Flexibilität!

4. **More comparisons.** Look at the pictures and then complete the sentences using the comparative or superlative forms with *than*, *as ... as* or *not as ... as*. Sometimes two answers are possible.

a) 

Oli is taller than Andy. (tall)

Andy isn't as tall as Oli. (tall)

b) 

My cat is ______________________ yours. (friendly)

Your cat ______________________ mine. (friendly)

c) 

I can run ____________________ you. (far)

You can't run __________________ me. (far)

d) 

Adam's computer is ____________________
Simon's. (expensive)

Nina's computer ______________________
Adam or Simon's. (expensive)

Nina's computer is ____________________
Adam and Simon's. (cheap)

e) 

Tom's face is _______________________
Jack's. (dirty)

Jack's face __________________________
Tom's. (dirty).

f) 

On Wednesdays I can get up ____________
_________ usual because school only starts at 8.20 a.m. (late)

On Wednesdays I don't have to get up ______
__________________ usual because school only starts at 8.20 a.m. (early)

5. Shopping. Kate and Tina have gone shopping. Complete their conversation.

KATE: My mum's given me some money for my birthday. I want to buy some clothes with it. Which jeans do you like, the black ones or the orange ones?

TINA: I think the black ones are ______________________ (nice).

KATE: Mmm, but they're also ______________________ (expensive).

TINA: Yes, but they're ______________________ (fashionable). What about the orange ones?

KATE: I don't know. Hey, what about those shoes? They're nice. They'll make me look ________________ (tall). Then no-one can say I'm ____________________ in the class any more! (small)

6. Postcard. Sam is in Scotland on an adventure holiday. He writes a postcard to a friend. Complete the card using each adjective once. You will have to change the adjectives as necessary using the comparative or superlative form. Sometimes more than one answer is possible: *exciting – good – difficult – friendly – nice – fun – high*

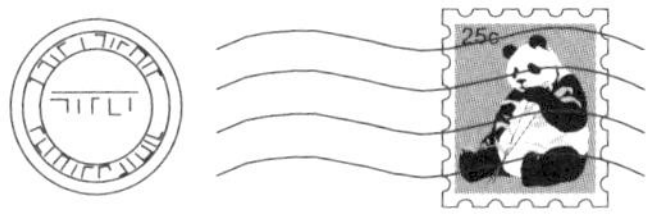

Dear Tom,
There are children from lots of different countries here. I went climbing yesterday. It was ____________ ____________ than I thought. We had to climb up very high. It's ______ ____________ mountain I've ever climbed. I'm going pony-trekking with most of the girls at the weekend. I think pony-trekking is ______ ____________ than mountain biking. I know you think mountain biking is ____________ but I love ponies. The ponies here are all right but my 'Black Beauty' is ____________ and ____________ and she's also faster. In fact she's ____________ ____________ pony in the world. See you on Monday.

Love
Sam

Tom Deane
13 Albany Way
CRANBROOK
Kent
TN17 1BC

7. Crossword. Using the clues to help you, complete the crossword.

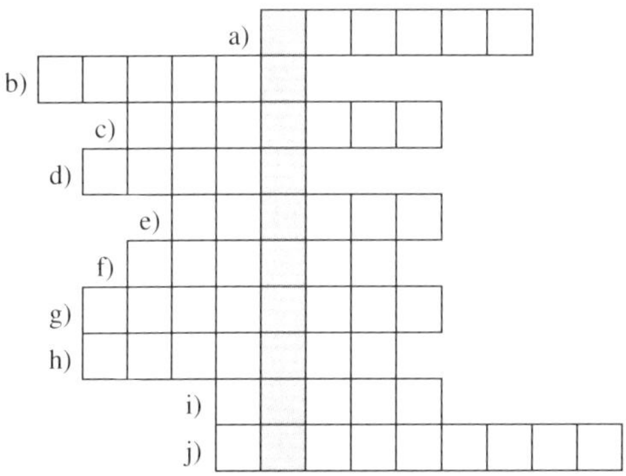

a) A Porsche is __________________ than a Fiat pinto.

b) I got a "3" for my English test this time. My mark was ______________ last time. I got a "1".

c) Jonathan doesn't do his homework or help at home and he never gets up on Saturdays before 10.30. He is one of the __________________ boys I know.

d) The opposite of b above.

e) Which river is __________________: the Nile or the Amazon?

f) It's much __________________ in winter in Britain than in Africa.

g) The opposite of "largest".

h) Tina weighs 40 kg, Ali only weighs 35. Tina is __________________ than Ali.

i) Pat gets DM 3.00 pocket money a week. Tom get DM 4.50 and Billy gets DM 6.00. Pat gets the __________________.

j) Some people think Claudia Schiffer is one of the __________________ women in the world.

The hidden word is: ____________________.

8. True sentences. Write true sentences.

a) horse/pony (large) → A horse is larger than a pony.

b) teenager/adult (old) → ____________________________

c) the Nile/the Rhein (long) → ____________________________

d) bench/sofa (comfortable) → ____________________________

e) path/road (wide) → ____________________________

f) DM 10/£10 (valuable) → ____________________________

g) bicycle/motor bike (dangerous) → ____________________________

h) £1 coin/5 p coin (small) → ____________________________

i) fresh fruit/tinned fruit (healthy) → ____________________________

9. How much do you know? Using the words below to help you, write sentences comparing the items in the pictures. Always start with the first word in each pair: *cold – further – long – heavy – valuable*

a) 

0° Celsius isn't as cold as 0° Fahrenheit.

b) 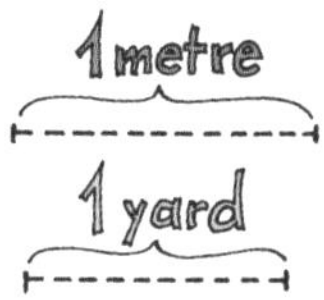

____

c) 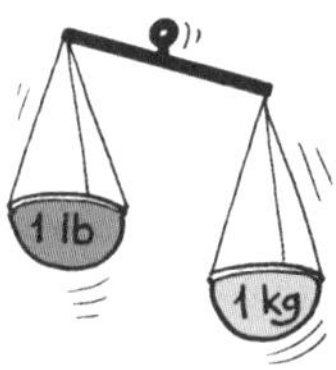

____

d) 

____

e) 

____

10. Personal statistics. Look at the information in the box. Then write sentences comparing the personal statistics about Emma, Oliver, Nathalie and William. Sometimes more than one answer is possible. Only use the words in brackets.

	Age	Height	Weight	IQ
Emma	15	1.75 m	60 kg	137
Oliver	14	1.80 m	66 kg	111
Nathalie	16	1.69 m	50 kg	125
William	13	1.72 m	58 kg	116

a) Emma/Oliver/Nathalie (heavy)

Oliver is the heaviest of the three.

b) Oliver/Emma (old)

c) Nathalie/Emma/Oliver (intelligent)

d) William/Nathalie (tall)

e) Emma/Oliver (heavy)

f) Oliver/Emma/William (tall)

g) William/Oliver/Nathalie (young)

h) William/Oliver (intelligent)

i) Emma/Nathalie/William (light)

j) Emma/Nathalie (intelligent)

5.2 Adjektive nach Verben der Sinneswahrnehmung

Wie du schon weißt, können Adjektive normalerweise nicht ein Verb näher beschreiben. Dafür sind immer die Adverbien zuständig. Dies sind z. B. Wörter wie *quickly, happily, terribly, well, immediately*.

Es gibt jedoch **fünf Verben, die immer ein Adjektiv bei sich haben** und kein Adverb. Dies sind die Verben der **Sinneswahrnehmung,** also *look, smell, sound, feel* und *taste*. Da die gleichen Verben auch verwendet werden können, um eine Aktivität zu bezeichnen, musst du hier besonders aufpassen.

11. Which verb? Use the pictures to help you complete the sentences.

a) 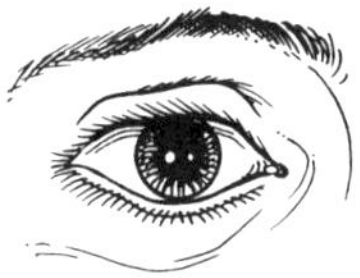

PAT: That strawberry cake ____________ good.

b) 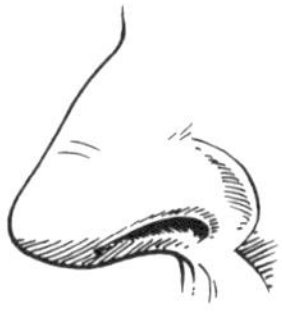

MICKY: Mmm. It_______________ fantastic.

c) 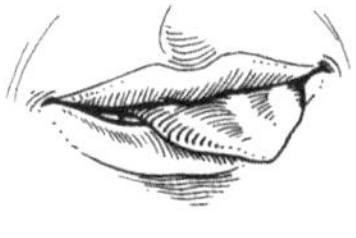

PAT: I bet it ________________ delicious. Let's buy some.

d) 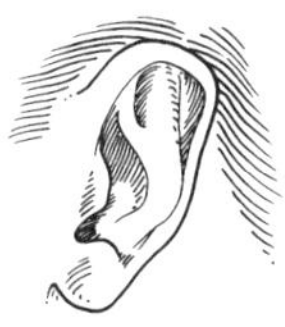

MICKY: That ____________________ like a good idea.

e) 

PAT: I ________________ hungry. I think I'll buy 4 slices.

MICKY: Don't, you'll ________________ sick afterwards!

Wie erkennst du Verben der Sinneswahrnehmung?

- Um herauszufinden, ob es sich wirklich um ein Verb der Sinneswahrnehmung handelt, mache den folgenden **Test:** Ersetze einfach das Verb durch eine Form von ***to be.*** Wenn das funktioniert, dann hast du es tatsächlich mit einem Verb der Sinneswahrnehmung zu tun. Und du erinnerst dich, was ein solches Verb bei sich hat? Richtig, dann steht immer ein **Adjektiv** (und natürlich **kein Adverb**)! Wenn der Test nicht funktioniert, bezeichnet das Verb eine Aktivität und hat ein Adverb bei sich.

  Beispiel: The milk {tastes / is} horrible. (Verb der Sinneswahrnehmung + Adjektiv)

- **Ausnahme:** *to feel*

  Wenn jemand dich fragt, wie es dir geht, anwortest du:

  Beispiel: I feel very well./I don't feel very well.

  Wenn *to feel* „tasten" bedeutet, wird das Verb ebenfalls mit einem Adverb beschrieben, und nicht mit einem Adjektiv.

  Beispiel: Blind people can feel very well with their hands.

12. Choose the right word. Complete the sentences by choosing one of the following words. Use each word **once only:** *carefully – horrible – loud – awful – well – stupid – slowly – carefully – funny – nice – ~~good~~*

a) That idea sounds ___good___.

b) You should look ________________ when you cross the road.

c) This meat tastes ________________.

d) Betty doesn't feel very ________________.

e) Caroline's boyfriend doesn't like her new hairstyle. He says it looks ____________________.

f) My mum has got lots of roses in her garden. I think they smell ____________________.

g) Simon felt his head ____________________. It was full of blood.

h) Turn your music down, it sounds too ____________________!

i) She tasted the soup____________________ because it was very hot.

j) Your trainers smell ________________! Put them in the washing machine NOW!

k) Your voice sounds ______________________. Have you got a cold?

13. Complete the following sentences using one of the verbs of the senses and an adjective.

a) My mum doesn't like the music I listen to: she says it ________________ ______________________.

b) I've got a headache. I ____.

c) This milk is old. It ____.

d) Do you like *The Spice Girls?* No, their music ____________________.

e) I love chocolate ice cream. It ____________________________.

f) My friend gave me some perfume for my birthday. It ______________.

g) Our teacher isn't at school today: she ________________________.

h) I like your new jeans, David. They ________________________.

i) My mum uses *Pulliweich.* My jumpers always ________________.

j) Are you all right Megan? You ____________________________. Shall I call the doctor?

6 Adverbien

Adverbien sind genauso wie Adjektive **beschreibende** Wörter, weil sie dir zusätzliche Informationen über bestimmte Wörter im Satz verschaffen. Ihre Aufgabe ist allerdings unterschiedlicher Art: Adjektive beschreiben Nomen, während **Adverbien Verben** näher beschreiben. Sie bringen also unter anderem zum Ausdruck, **wie** etwas gemacht wird.

Beispiele: Trish is a quick reader. (Adjektiv)
Trish reads quickly. (Adverb)

Rund ums Adverb

Wie bildest du Adverbien?

Anders als du es im Deutschen kennen gelernt hast, unterscheiden sich im Englischen Adjektive und Adverbien meist auch in der Form voneinander.

- Die meisten Adverbien bildest du, indem du ein *-ly* an das Adjektiv hängst.
  Beispiel: quick → quickly
- Endet das Adjektiv auf ***-able/-ible,*** dann musst du aus dem *-e* ein *-y* machen.
  Beispiel: suitable → suitably
- Endet das Adjektiv auf ***-y,*** dann musst du aus dem *-y* ein *-i* machen und schließlich noch unser bekanntes *-ly* anhängen.
  Beispiel: heavy → heavily
- Hat das Adjektiv aber ein **Doppel-*ll*** am Ende, dann musst du einfach noch ein *-y* hinzufügen.
  Beispiel: full → fully

- Einige Adverbien werden **nicht regelmäßig** gebildet. Du weißt schon, was das bedeutet: Auswendig lernen!

Beispiele:	fast	→	<u>fast</u>	This is a fast train.	The train went <u>fast</u>.
	good	→	<u>well</u>	She's a good worker.	She works <u>well</u>.
	hard	→	<u>hard</u>	The work is hard.	They worked <u>hard</u>.
	late	→	<u>late</u>	Maria is often late.	She often arrives <u>late</u>.

- Einige Adjektive, die auf *-ly* enden, haben **keine** passende Adverbform. Hier musst du dann eine sogenannte **Adverbialphrase** *(adverbial phrase)* benutzen, oder ein **anderes Adverb** mit ähnlicher Bedeutung finden. Die passende **Präposition** dazu nicht vergessen! Beispiele hierfür sind *friendly, lovely, silly, lonely, difficult.*

Beispiele: Tina's horse is <u>friendly</u>. (Adjektiv)
He often looks at me <u>in a friendly way</u>. (Adverbialphrase)

You've got a <u>lovely</u> voice. (Adjektiv)
You sing <u>in a lovely way</u>/<u>beautifully</u>. (Adverbialphrase/Adverb)

- Nach den Verben *to grow* (wachsen) und *to become* (werden) kann **kein Adverb** stehen. Wie *to be* und die *Verben der Wahrnehmung* (siehe S. 49) werden diese beiden Verben in Verbindung mit einem **Adjektiv** benutzt.

Beispiele: The weather <u>became</u> <u>stormy</u> as they got near the coast. (Adjektiv)
Eve <u>ran</u> <u>stormily</u> out of her father's study. (Adverb)

It was past midnight. Amelia's mother started <u>to grow</u> <u>nervous</u>. (Adjektiv)
Amelia <u>spoke</u> <u>nervously</u> to her mother from a friend's house: she had missed the last bus home. (Adverb)

1. **Getting it right.** Complete the following table by writing in the correct English form of the adjective and adverb.

German	adjective	adverb
durstig		
schnell	quick/fast	quickly/fast
möglich		
spät		
freundlich		
ruhig		
hungrig		
böse/verärgert		
hart/schwer		
gut		
nervös		

2. **Adjective or adverb?** Decide whether an adjective or adverb should complete these sentences. Choose from the table in Exercise 1. Use each adjective/adverb only once.

a) If you run quickly, you can catch the fast train to London.

b) This cake tastes ______________. Who made it?

c) On Monday morning Danny was very ________________: he had to do ______________ in his English test this time.

d) Two days later: "I don't believe it! It's not __________________", said Danny as he got his English test back. "All that _______________ work and I only got a 4. My mum's going to be _______________ when I tell her."

e) The little mouse looked _________________ out of his hole. Where was that cat?

f) "I'm sorry, I can't _________________ mend your bike before Tuesday. I've been working ______________ all week and I still haven't finished.

Rund um die Steigerung von Adverbien

Wie steigerst du Adverbien?

- **Einsilbige Adverbien:** Du musst einfach die Steigerungsendungen *-er/ -est* an die Grundform anhängen.

Beispiele:	hard	harder	hardest
	fast	faster	fastest

Tom worked hard. Jim worked harder. Betty worked hardest.

- **Adverbien mit zwei oder mehr Silben:** Setze einfach das Wörtchen *more* vor die Grundform des Adverbs, um den Komparativ *(comparative)* zu bilden und *most* um den Superlativ *(superlative)* zu bilden.

Beispiele:	quickly	more quickly	most quickly
	happily	more happily	most happily

My sister drives quickly. My mother drives more quickly. My grandmother drives most quickly.

Ausnahme:	early	earlier	earliest

- Einige Adverbien haben **unregelmäßige Steigerungsformen**. Wie immer musst du diese auswendig lernen!

Beispiele:	well	better	best
	badly	worse	worst
	little	less	least
	much	more	most
	far	farther	farthest

Betty sings well. Her brother Tom sings better. Her friend Sally sings best.

Das Gegenteil von *more* ist *less* und das Gegenteil von *most* demzufolge *least.* Diese Formen brauchst du, wenn du noch weitere Komparative und Superlative bilden willst.

3. Word chains. Find adjectives in the box which make a pair (opposites) and then form a chain: adjective/adverb/comparative/superlative.

~~slow~~	easy	loud	good
happy	late	sad	stupid
quiet	careful	dangerous	~~fast~~
bad	hard	early	clever

a) slow → slowly → more slowly → most slowly
↕
fast → fast → faster → fastest

b) ______ → ______ → ______ → ______
↕
______ → ______ → ______ → ______

c) ______ → ______ → ______ → ______
↕
______ → ______ → ______ → ______

d) ______ → ______ → ______ → ______
↕
______ → ______ → ______ → ______

e) ______ → ______ → ______ → ______
↕
______ → ______ → ______ → ______

f) ______ → ______ → ______ → ______
↕
______ → ______ → ______ → ______

g) ______ → ______ → ______ → ______
↕
______ → ______ → ______ → ______

h) ______ → ______ → ______ → ______
↕
______ → ______ → ______ → ______

4. Choices. Choose a suitable adverb from the pair of adjectives in brackets and then complete the sentences using the correct form of the **same adverb.**

a) 

Marcia drives carefully but her grandmother drives more carefully. (careful/dangerous)

b) 

Marie usually arrives at school ____________ but her friend Susan comes always ____________________. (late/early).

c) 

A tortoise moves ____________________ but a snail moves ________________________ (fast/slow)

d) 

Bobby didn't work ________________ for the English test and got a bad mark. His friend Steve worked _________________ in the class and got the best mark. (much/little)

e) 

Nick usually does very ______________ in the 100 m race but this time he did much ______________. (bad/good)

f) 

The thief broke into the bank ______________ but he didn't see the policeman behind him who was waiting even ______________ for him to finish before he arrested him. (quiet/loud)

5. **Practising comparisons.** Choose the correct adjective or adverb form of the words in brackets ( ) to complete the sentences: + = standard form; ++ = comparative; +++ = superlative.

a) Belinda is very _good_ (+ good) at athletics: she can throw the discus _further than_ (++ far) most of the boys.

b) Tom answered his teacher rather ______________ (+ impolite). Mr Jackdaw said, "Tom, if you don't speak ______________ (++ polite) to me, I'll have to give you extra homework. I know you can be ______________ (++ sensible) when you want to be."

c) Rob hit the ball ______________ (+ powerful) to his partner Jonah. Suddenly the ball came back at him even ______________ (++ powerful): Jonah was ______________ (+++ good) player in the team.

d) Judy worked ______________ (+++ fast) she had ever worked in her life. She had to finish her homework ______________ (++ early) than usual because she was meeting her new boyfriend, Simon, at the bus stop at 6.20 p.m.

Rund um den Vergleich mit Adverbien

Adverbien können, wie die Adjektive (siehe S. 55), mit ihren Komparativformen verschiedene Formen von **Gleichheit und Ungleichheit** ausdrücken.

Beispiele: I can run faster than you. (Ungleichheit beim einsilbigen Adverb)
You can run as fast as Jack. (Gleichheit)
Jack can't run as fast as Adrian. (‚negative' Ungleichheit)
Adrian can run more quickly than any of us.
(‚positive' Ungleichheit beim mehrsilbigen Adverb)
We all run less quickly than Adrian.
(‚negative' Ungleichheit beim mehrsilbigen Adverb)

6. Sports – from adjective to adverb. Re-write the following sentences so that the comparative form includes an adverb and not an adjective. Use the words and signs in brackets ( ) in the new sentences: ↑ = positive Ungleichheit; ↓ = negative Ungleichheit; ↔ = Gleichheit; ??? = frei.

a) Steffi Graf is still a good tennis player. (**1.** Martina Hingis + ???/ **2.** Martina Hingis + ↓;)
She can still play tennis better than Martina Hingis.
Martina Hingis can't play tennis as well as her.

b) Mika Häkkinen is sometimes a dangerous driver. (Michael Schumacher + ↔)
He sometimes ______

c) Jonathan Edwards is the best triple jumper in the world. (**1.** anyone else + far + ???/**2.** him + far + ↓)
He can ______
No-one ______

d) Arsenal is a successful English football club. Newcastle United is not successful at the moment. (**1.** play + ↑/**2.** play + ↓)
Arsenal is playing ______
Newcastle United is not playing ______

e) Grit Breuer is a fast 400 m runner. (**1.** ??? + most other runners/ **2.** most + her + ↓)
She ____
____
____

f) The New Zealand *All Blacks* rugby team is strong. (the Australian *Wallabies* team + play + ↓)
____
____

✷ **7.** **Braveheart.** Fill in the gaps in this text about a famous Scottish hero using the correct form of the given adjectives/ adverbs.

Sir William Wallace is one of ______________________ (famous) Scottish heroes. He was born about 1272 and died ______________________ (brave) for Scotland on 23 August 1305. In 1296 Scotland had no king anymore: King John of Scotland was in exile in France. King Edward I of England thought he could beat the Scots ____________________ (easy) he had beaten the Welsh so that both small countries would be under English power. But the Scots had a very ______________________ (strong) leader – Sir William Wallace – and they fought ___________________________ (successful) the Welsh.

The Scots fought many battles but their ________________ (important) ones were in 1297. In the first they fought ___________________ (fierce) and killed the sheriff of Lanark who at the time was English. Later that year they sieged the English at Dundee on the east coast. The English armies were a lot _________________ (big) the Scottish ones but the Scots were fighting for their freedom. Because Wallace's wife and brother had already been killed by them he had nothing to lose: he was afraid of nothing, he was a 'brave heart'.

In Stirling, near Glasgow, the Scots fought their ___________________ (brave) battle for freedom. King Edward's army was the biggest (10,000 foot soldiers and 500 on horses) and __________________ (good) but the Scots knew the land ______________________ (good) the English. King Edward's men never got ______________________ (far) Stirling Bridge because the River Forth divided his army and Wallace _______________ (clever) used this _________________ (difficult) situation. The Scots won and more than half of the English army died.

In 1293 Wallace fought _________________ (successful) and finally lost to the English at the Battle of Falkirk. For many years he hid in France but in 1305 he returned and was discovered. After his trial in London he was sentenced to death – a ________________ (terrible) death. But, people in Scotland did not forget the man with the ______________ (big) two-handed sword and they didn't stop fighting. Finally in 1314, under King Robert I of Scotland, who is much _______________ (good) known as Robert the Bruce, they _______________ (successful) beat the English at the famous Battle of Bannockburn. Scotland became independent.

Scotland has not forgotten her hero. In Stirling The Wallace Monument stands high on a hill for everyone to see. This 'museum' is small but ________________ (modern) many other _________________ (large) ones. It uses videos and other special effects to make visitors feel they are really living what is happening and Wallace's sword is also there.

7 Zeitformen des Verbs

Die Zeitformen des Verbs sind ein Hauptbestandteil der bisher erarbeiteten Grammatik und sie werden auch weiterhin, solange du Englisch lernst, dein ständiger Begleiter sein! Es gibt Zeiten, die dir keine Probleme bereiten werden, andere wiederum können mehr Schwierigkeiten machen, z. B. wenn das Deutsche nur eine Zeitform aufweist, während das Englische zwei vorweisen kann (z. B. *simple present, present progressive).*
Genau wie beim Vokabeln lernen, kannst du eine Zeitform nicht über Nacht beherrschen, sondern du musst versuchen, so regelmäßig wie möglich mit ihnen zu arbeiten. Eine gute Möglichkeit, sie relativ schnell in den Griff zu bekommen, ist z. B. das Anfertigen einer **übersichtlichen Tabelle** für die **wichtigsten Hilfsverben** (*to be, to have, to do*) und **ein regelmäßiges Verb.** Hier siehst du, wie eine Tabelle für ein regelmäßiges Verb aussehen könnte:

	Aussageform	Verneinung	Frage
simple present	I* play	I *don't* play	*Do* I play?
present progressive	I *am* play*ing*	I'*m not* play*ing*	*Am* I play*ing*?
simple past	I play*ed*	I *didn't* play	*Did* I play?
past progressive	I *was* play*ing*	I *wasn't* play*ing*	*Was* I play*ing*?
present perfect simple	I *have* play*ed*	I *haven't* play*ed*	*Have* I play*ed*?
present perfect progressive	I *have been* play*ing*	I *haven't been* play*ing*	*Have* I *been* play*ing*?
past perfect simple	I *had* play*ed*	I *hadn't* play*ed*	*Had* I play*ed*?
past perfect progressive	I *had been* play*ing*	I *hadn't been* play*ing*	*Had* I *been* play*ing*?
will-future	I *will* play	I *won't* play	*Will* I play?
going-to-future	I *am going to* play	I'*m not going to* play	*Am* I *going to* play?

* Du musst in deiner Tabelle natürlich die anderen Personen (du, er, sie, es etc.) noch ergänzen.

7.1 *simple present* und *present progressive*

simple present und *present progressive* sind Zeitformen der **Gegenwart.** Ihre jeweilige Verwendung unterliegt bestimmten Regeln.

Rund um die Verwendung der *simple*-Form

Du benutzt das *simple present*, um Umstände zum Ausdruck zu bringen, die wahr sind und sich nicht verändern:

- **Unveränderliche Sachverhalte:** Es besteht kein Grund zur Annahme, dass sich irgend etwas verändern wird.

  Beispiele: We live in a small village.
  Nesrin comes from Turkey.

- **Angewohnheiten, regelmäßige Aktivitäten**

  Beispiele: I drink a lot of milk.
  She never eats ice-cream.
  How often do you go to the dentist?

- Als **allgemein wahr** und **unveränderlich** erachtete Begebenheiten, die regelmäßig vorkommen.

  Beispiele: The earth goes round the sun.
  The sun rises in the east.
  The train leaves at 6.10.

- **Wissenschaftliche Erkenntnisse**

  Beispiel: Water boils at 100 °C.

- **Allgemeinplätze**

  Beispiele: Cats catch mice.
  English people drink a lot of tea.

Im Folgenden findest du einige nützliche **Schlüsselwörter,** die dir helfen sollen, das *simple present* zu erkennen und zu benutzen.

- **Adverbien der Häufigkeit** wie z. B. *always, usually, often, never*

  Beispiele: Ken always arrives at school first.
  Paula never plays with her little sister.

- Andere **Zeitangaben** wie z. B. *on Tuesday(s), daily, every week, once a month/monthly, twice a year*

  Beispiele: On Tuesdays I've got football practice.
  Rose has a music lesson once a week.

Rund um die Verwendung der *progressive*-Form

Du benutzt das *present progressive (continuous)*, um auszudrücken, dass

- du eine Handlung jetzt gerade im Moment ausführst: eine **zeitlich begrenzte** Handlung, die vor dem Zeitpunkt des Sprechens begonnen hat, weiter andauert und noch nicht beendet ist.

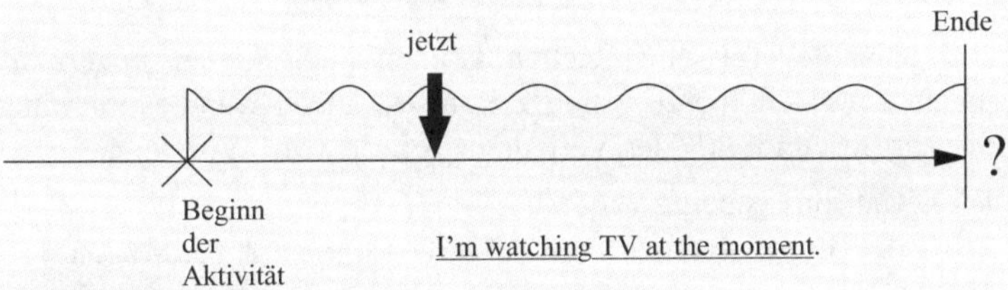

- die baldige Beendigung eines Zustands/einer Aktivität zu erwarten ist, d. h. wenn es sich um einen **begrenzten Zeitraum** handelt.

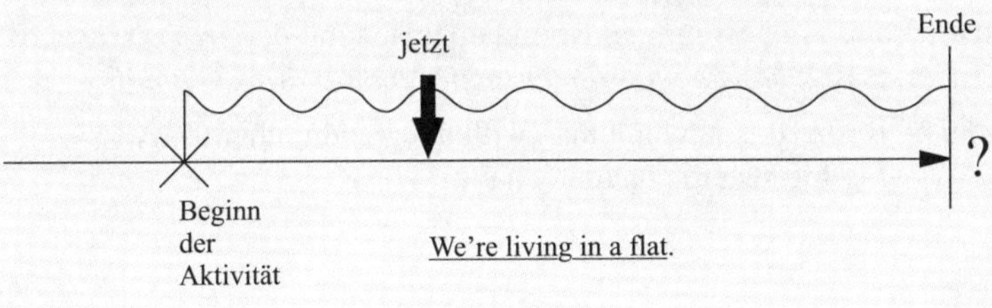

- du irgendeiner Tätigkeit **regelmäßig** (aber nicht unbedingt jetzt gerade) und nur für eine **begrenzte Zeitdauer** nachgehst.

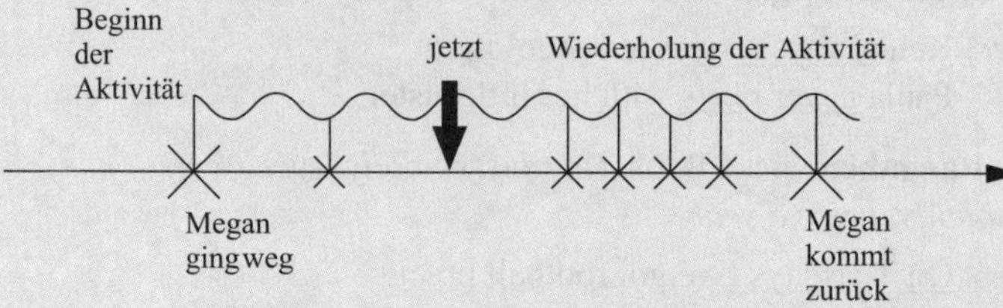

I'm feeding Megan's rabbit while she's on holiday.

- Wichtige **Schlüsselwörter** sind: *now, at the moment.*

Besondere Verwendungsmöglichkeiten und Ausnahmen

- Im Zusammenhang mit *always* bezeichnet das *present progressive* eine **bedauernswerte Angewohnheit.** Eine Tat oder ein Vorkommnis wiederholt sich ziemlich oft und der Sprecher ist darüber verärgert.

  Beispiel: My grandfather is always losing his keys.

- Einige sogenannte **statische Verben** können nicht in der *progressive* Form benutzt werden, hierzu gehört z. B. ***to be,*** ausser wenn es mit einem Adjektiv zur Beschreibung des Verhaltens benutzt wird. Vergleiche:

  Beispiele: Catriona is being very silly.
  (Dies ist nur von kurzer Dauer: sie verhält sich gerade jetzt im Moment albern.)

  Catriona is silly.
  (Dies ist ihr normales Verhalten, sie ist immer so.)

- ***to have*** wird nur in bestimmten Nominalphrasen mit der *progressive form* verwendet, z. B. *a bath/a baby/lunch/a nice time/a drink/a holiday.*

  Beispiele: Rasheed is having lunch with his grandmother today.
  My big sister is having a baby.

1. Sentence analysis. Read the following sentences and then decide what sort of *present progressive* or *simple present* they are. Complete the table. One of the sentences can be used twice!

a) Louise is watering Mrs Price's plants because she's in hospital.

b) Toby is living with his grandparents while his parents move.

c) Some people never clean their teeth.

d) Janine is borrowing my bike until she gets a new one.

e) Wait a minute. I'm cleaning my shoes.

f) In autumn most trees lose all their leaves. (two possibilities here)

g) Most children in Britain wear uniforms to school.

h) You always make such delicious cakes.

i) Trudy sings beautifully.

j) "Jack, you're being impolite to your aunt. Say sorry now!"

k) "Why are you always borrowing my lipstick?", said Chris to her younger sister, Tammy.

l) The news on BBC 1 is at 6 p.m. and 9 p.m.

m) Red and blue make purple.

n) Chinese and Japanese people have got black hair.

o) Jon is having a nice time on holiday.

p) My mother does the washing every Monday morning.

present progressive				
zeitlich begrenzte Handlung	zeitlich begrenzter Zeitraum	zeitlich begrenzte Gewohnheit	bedauernswerte Angewohnheit	Ausnahme
		a		

simple present				
unveränderliche Sachverhalte	Angewohnheit, regelmäßige Aktivität	allgemein wahre Begebenheit	wissenschaftliche Erkenntnis	Allgemeinplatz

Wie bildest du das *present progressive?*

- Der normale **Aussagesatz** des ***present progressive*** wird gebildet mit der Präsensform des Hilfsverbs *to be* + Infinitiv + *-ing*.

  Beispiel: I am working hard at the moment.

- Die **Verneinung** des ***present progressive*** bildest du, indem du *not* nach dem Hilfsverb einsetzt.

  Beispiele: Dana isn't working at home tonight.
  We aren't enjoying the party very much.

- Die **Frageform** des ***present progressive*** bildest du, indem du Subjekt und Hilfsverb vertauschst (Inversion).

  Beispiele: Are they working?
  Why are you hurrying?

Wie bildest du das *simple present?*

- Die **Aussageform** des ***simple present*** bildest du genauso wie den **Infinitiv**, nur musst du in der **3. Person Singular** ein *-s* anfügen.

  Beispiele: I work hard before a test.
  Dana works hard all year.

- Die **Verneinung** des ***simple present*** bildest du mit den Präsensformen des Hilfsverbs *to do + not + infinitive* (ohne *to*) des Vollverbs.

  Beispiele: I do not work late at night.
  Miranda does not work here anymore.

- Die **Frage** des ***simple present*** bildest du mit der Präsensform von *to do* in der Frageform (*do/does* + Subjekt) + Infinitiv (ohne *to*) des Vollverbs.

  Beispiele: Do you work in a factory?
  Does the machine work?

2. **Over to you.** Complete the following sentences using either the *present progressive* or the *present simple* tense.

   a) Look! That man (try) is trying to steal a bike.

   b) "Can you play the guitar?"
   "No, but I (learn) ________________. My aunt (teach) ______________ me."

   c) My grandmother (live) __________________ in Glasgow. She was born there and has never lived anywhere else. Where (your grandparents + live) ____?

   d) Moira's computer (not work) __________________ at the moment.

   e) My mother (grow + usually) _____________________ lots of flowers in the garden but this year she (not grow) ______________________ any.

   f) Ed (learn) ______________________ his part for the school play. It (be) _______________ hard work because he (have got) ________________ the main part.

   g) British pupils (go) __________________ to school in the afternoon.

   h) Hurry up, Gina. The train (come) __________________!

i) The moon (go) ___________________ round the earth.

j) (it + ever + snow) ____________________________ in Australia?

k) The government (be) ____________________ a little nervous because the number of people without jobs (grow) ________________.

l) Michael Owen (play) ___________________ football brilliantly.

m) Charlotte (get) ____________________ £1 every week from her grandpa.

Rund um die Zeitform bei Verben der Wahrnehmung

- Es gibt fünf Verben der Wahrnehmung: *to see, feel, smell, taste und hear.* Wenn du etwas siehst, fühlst, riechst, schmeckst oder hörst, dann tust du dies normalerweise **unbewusst**, ohne eigenes dazutun, ohne weiter darüber nachzudenken. Du führst hier keine wirkliche Aktivität aus.

  Beispiele: We see the old man everyday when we walk to school.
  This jumper feels soft.
  That milk smells bad.
  "Mum, this cake tastes delicious!"
  When my dog hears the phone ring he always barks.

- Wenn du eine **unbewusste Wahrnehmung** beschreiben willst, dann musst du eins dieser Verben im *simple present* verwenden. Willst du aber einen Vorgang beschreiben, den du irgendwie **kontrollieren kannst**, handelt es sich also um eine **bewusste Handlungen,** dann musst du ein **anderes Verb** einsetzen: ***see*** → *watch* oder *look*; ***hear*** → *listen.* Diese alternativ verfügbaren Verben können dann natürlich auch im *present progressive* stehen.Vergleiche hierzu die folgenden Verbpaare:

  Beispiele: We listen to the radio when we are in the car.
  I'm listening to the CD you gave me: it's great.
  I can't hear you. The music is too loud. (Verb der Wahrnehmung)

  Before I cross a road in Britain I always look right, then left and then right again.
  I'm looking where you said but I can't find the key.
  Ah, now I can see it. (Verb der Wahrnehmung)

Darfst du die Verben der Wahrnehmung auch einmal im *present progressive* benutzen?

- In einigen Fällen kannst du die Verben der Wahrnehmung auch im *present progressive* benutzen. Ihre **Bedeutung verändert** sich in diesem Fall jedoch: sie bezeichnen dann **bewusste Handlungen.** *to hear* und *to see* werden nicht sehr häufig auf diese Weise benutzt.

  Beispiele: Dad is feeling the paint to see if it is already dry.
  (Hier bedeutet *to feel* „anfassen".)

  Mum's smelling the roses in your garden. She loves roses.
  (Hier bedeutet *to smell* „etwas beschnuppen".)

  The chef is tasting the soup to see if there is enough pepper in it.
  (Hier bedeutet *to taste* „versuchen /probieren".)

Gibt es noch andere Verben, die normalerweise nicht im *present progressive* stehen können?

- Verben, die ein **Gefühl** zum Ausdruck bringen wie z. B. *to love, like, hate, want, prefer* können nur in der Form des *simple present* benutzt werden.

  Beispiele: I love American ice–cream.
  I want to go camping this summer.
  I prefer *N'Sync's* music.

- Verben, die **gedankliche Vorgänge** beschreiben wie z. B. *to believe, forget, know, remember, understand* können **nicht** im *present progressive* stehen.

  Beispiele: Many people believe that school days are the best.
  Serena forgets many things but I still like her.
  Do you know what the highest mountain in the world is?
  Old people easily remember what life was like when they were children.
  I don't understand this. Can you please explain it again?

3. About yourself. Answer the following questions about yourself. Write **full sentences**.

a) What's your name? My name is Lesley Croucher.

b) Where do you live? ______________________

c) How many brothers and sisters have you got? ______________________

d) Which subjects at school do you prefer?

____

e) Which subjects at school do you not like?

____

f) Do you play a musical instrument? Yes, ______________ / No, ______________.

If yes, how often do you practise a week?

____

g) What music do you listen to?

____

h) Are you in a sports club? Yes, ______________ / No, ______________.

If yes, how many times a week do you go to the club?

____

i) What time do you get up and go to bed on school days?

____

4. A letter home. Molly is on holiday on a farm. She writes a short letter to her parents. Using either the *present progressive* or the *present simple* complete her letter.

Thursday

Dear Mum and Dad

I (have) ________________ a wonderful time here with Uncle John and Aunt Maureen. They (have got) ________________ lots of animals and they said I can feed the new lambs whose mother died. Their names (be) ________________ Fluffy and Clarry. I (feed) ________________ them five times a day with a baby's bottle. David (stay) ________________ with a friend at the moment so I (do) ________________ his job too until Sunday: the chickens. I (prefer) ________________ the lambs because they (be) ________ more interesting. Susie's new pony Dash (jump) ________________ very well. She's in a competition with him on Saturday. At the moment we (get) ____________________ everything ready. We started yesterday and we won't be finished until late on Friday. We (have got) ________________ so much to do. (remember + you) ________________ Susie's friend, Juliet? She has moved and (live) ________________ in another village further away so we can't go and see her.

You won't believe it: because the cockerel (make + always) ________ ____________ so much noise I (wake up) ______________ before six o'clock every morning! That's one thing I won't miss at home: you (know) ________________ how I (hate) ________________ early mornings. See you on Wednesday. Lots of love

Molly

5. Translation. Translate the following text into English. Take special care with the *present tenses.*

Fred ist gerade bei seiner Großmutter zu Hause (in ihrer Wohnung), weil seine Mutter im Krankenhaus ist. Normalerweise wohnt er zusammen mit seiner Mutter, seiner Schwester und ihrer Katze Mog in einem Haus. Fred geht in die 7. Klasse. Er geht nicht besonders gerne in die Schule, aber er mag die Schulband. Er spielt Schlagzeug und er spielt sehr gut. Aber Großmutters Nachbarn denken, dass er zu laut spielt. Im Moment übt er für das Weihnachtskonzert seiner Schule. Er probt dreimal die Woche. Die Nachbarn sagen oft: „Dieser Junge! Er spielt andauernd auf seinem Schlagzeug. Warum macht er nicht seine Hausaufgaben, das ist doch viel leiser, oder nicht?“

7.2 Die Wiedergabe der Zukunft mit dem *present progressive* und mit *going-to*

Es gibt Zeitformen, die mehrere grammatische Funktionen haben. Dazu gehört auch das *present progressive:* Du kannst es dazu benutzen, um über die Gegenwart zu reden. In besonderen Fällen kannst du damit aber auch Zukünftiges ausdrücken. Dies bedeutet also, dass du zwar beidesmal **dieselbe Form des Verbs** bildest, diese aber zu **unterschiedlichen Zwecken** nutzt.

Wann kannst du mit dem *present progressive* über die Zukunft reden?

- Wenn du über **Verabredungen oder Pläne** redest, die du für zukünftige Zwecke gemacht hast oder über Dinge, die du zu tun beabsichtigst.

  Beispiele: What are you doing tomorrow afternoon?
  ≈ I'm playing football.

- Sollte es nicht ganz klar sein, ob du über die Zukunft redest, musst du ein passendes **Adverb der Zeit** mit einbeziehen, wie z. B. *next weekend, tomorrow, this evening, tonight.* Vergleiche:

  Beispiele: What are you doing? (Was machst du gerade?)
  (Das *present progressive* bezieht sich hier auf die Gegenwart.)
  What are you doing tomorrow? (Was machst du morgen?)
  (Das Adverb zeigt, dass ein Bezug zur Zukunft besteht.)

- Die Adverbien der Zeit (anders als die der Häufigkeit, die im allgemeinen mit dem *simple present* benutzt werden) stehen gewöhnlich am **Ende eines Satzes,** nämlich nach dem Verb. Zur besonderen Hervorhebung können sie aber auch ganz am Anfang stehen.

  Beispiele: Colin usually plays football on Fridays but this week he is playing on Saturday.
  Are you playing hockey tonight?

6. What day? What are these children planning to do this week? Match up each child with the activity (either a verb on its own or a verb + noun construction) which starts with the same letter of the alphabet as the child's name. Then write a sentence, starting with 'Tuesday's child'.

a) Moira is making a cake on Monday.

b) ______________________________

c) ______________________________ in Wales ______________

d) ______________________________

e) ______________________________

f) ______________________________

g) ______________________________

7. A holiday. Today is Saturday. Your friend, Pip, is planning to go cycling around England very soon. You ask him about his plans: use the words in brackets to make your questions. Write Pip's answers using his diary to help you.

a) (when/to leave) When are you leaving? – I'm leaving on Monday.

b) (to go/alone) ______________________________

____

c) (where/to meet) ______________________________

____

d) (where/first day/to go) ______________________________

____

e) (how long/to stay/Canterbury) ______________________________

____

f) (name/last town/to cycle to) ______________________________

____

g) (when/home/to come) ______________________________

____

Wann benutzt du *to be going to* + Infinitiv zum Ausdruck der Zukunft?

- Du setzt ***to be going to*** ein, um über etwas zu reden, was du **beschlossen** hast zu tun, oder was du noch zu tun **beabsichtigst.** Allerdings sagt dieses Verb nicht aus, dass die nötigen Vorkehrungen bereits getroffen worden sind. Dies ist der Unterschied zum *present progressive* zum Ausdruck der Zukunft: Der Plan existiert nur in deinem Kopf, ist noch nicht ausgereift und du hast auch noch nichts unternommen, um ihn auszuführen. Vergleiche:

Beispiele: I'm playing tennis on Saturday.

(Der Platz ist bereits reserviert, du bist fest verabredet.)

I'm going to play tennis on Saturday.

(Du hast beschlossen, wie du deinen Samstag verbringen willst, hast aber noch keine Verabredungen oder sonstige Vorkehrungen getroffen.)

In vielen Fällen sind die beiden Konstruktionen '*present progressive* zum Ausdruck der Zukunft' und '*to be going to* + infinitive' untereinander **austauschbar:** Die Bedeutungsunterschiede sind so gering, dass sie mehr oder weniger irrelevant sind.

7.3 *simple past* oder *present perfect?*

Mit diesen beiden Zeitformen kannst du über die **Vergangenheit** sprechen, aber ganz anders als im Deutschen, sind die Regeln zur Benutzung der verschiedenen Formen streng einzuhalten: Ihre Bedeutung und ihr Verhältnis zur Vergangenheit stellen sich sehr unterschiedlich dar. Das ***present perfect*** ist nämlich im Unterschied zum deutschen Perfekt **keine reine Zeitform der Vergangenheit.** Mit dem *present perfect* kannst du vielmehr ausdrücken, dass eine Handlung in der Vergangenheit begonnen hat und bis in die Gegenwart andauert oder zumindest einen deutlichen **Einfluss auf die Gegenwart** ausübt.

Rund um das *simple past*

Wann benutzt du das *simple past?*

Du verwendest das *simple past,*

- um über etwas zu reden, das zu einer **bestimmten Zeit in der Vergangenheit** vor sich ging und keinen Bezug zur Gegenwart hat. Du gebrauchst das *simple past,* wenn du von abgeschlossenen Handlungen sprichst. Typische **Erkennungsmerkmale,** die dir anzeigen, dass das *simple past* zu benutzen ist, sind **Zeitangaben in der Vergangenheit,** z. B. *1066*, oder auch **adverbiale Zeitbestimmungen** wie *yesterday, last year, a week ago, last Tuesday.*

  Beispiele: I saw Carrie yesterday.
  Gill went on holiday to Spain last year.
  The Battle of Hastings was in 1066.
  Jack was late for school this morning because he only woke up at 8.30.

- um über Ereignisse zu reden, die **ständig oder wiederholt in der Vergangenheit** stattfanden, z. B. eine Angewohnheit oder regelmäßige Tätigkeit, aber jetzt nicht mehr ausgeübt werden.

Beispiele: Dinosaurs lived on the earth. (but they don't nowadays)
When my mother was twenty she rode a motorbike.
(Sie ist nicht mehr 20 und fährt nicht mehr Motorrad.)
People used candles to light their houses.
(Heutzutage gibt es Elektrizität.)

- um **Geschichten** in der Vergangenheit zu erzählen.

Beispiel: A man walked into a bank and said, "Hands up!"

- als Zeitindikator in Sätzen, die durch ***when*** eingeleitet werden. Die Aktivität, die durch *when* eingeführt wird, liefert den Hintergrund zur Hauptaktivität.

Beispiel: My grandfather always sang when he worked.

Rund um das *present perfect*

Wann benutzt du das *present perfect?*

Das *present perfect* verwendest du,

- um einen nicht **abgeschlossenen Vorgang** zu beschreiben, bei dem sich weder der Handelnde noch das Ergebnis ändern. Diese Vorgänge werden häufig durch die Wörter *for* oder *since* eingeführt (vgl. hierzu bitte die zusätzlichen Regeln auf S. 92 im Abschnitt *present perfect progressive*).

Beispiele: We've lived in Penzance since 1989.
They've had a dog for years.

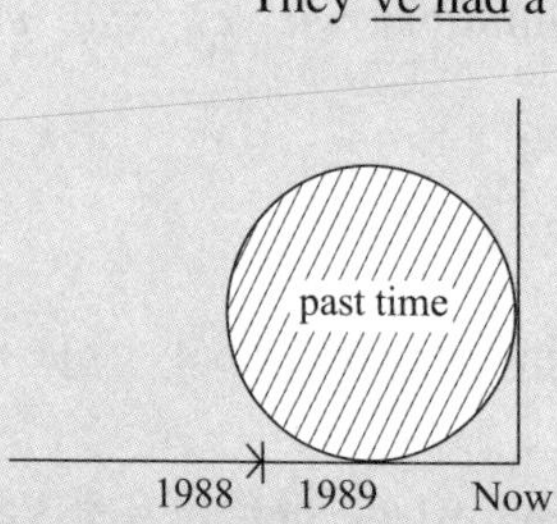

We lived in Canterbury until the end of 1988.
(Wir wohnen nicht mehr dort).

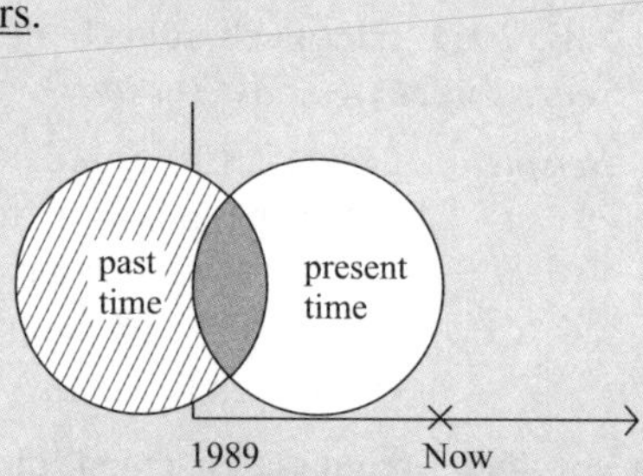

We have lived in Penzance since 1989.
(1989 zogen wir hier ein und wir wohnen heute immer noch hier.)

- um einen Vorgang zu beschreiben, der zu einer **bestimmten Zeit** stattfand und noch **nicht endgültig abgeschlossen** ist. Vergleiche:

  Beispiele: We've played tennis this morning. (Es ist noch 'heute Morgen'.)
  We played tennis this morning. (Jetzt ist es nach 12 Uhr Mittags.)

- um einen Vorgang zu erläutern, der sich kürzlich in der Vergangenheit abspielte, dessen **Folgen** aber immer noch sichtbar sind.

  Beispiele: I've mended your bicycle for you. (Jetzt funktioniert es.)
  Someone has broken the window. (Die Scherben liegen noch herum.)

8. Sentence analysis. Read the following sentences, decide under which category they belong and complete the table.

Simple Past				
Bestimmte Zeit in der Vergangenheit	Ereignis, das ständig in der Vergangenheit stattgefunden hat	Wiederholtes Ereignis (Angewohnheit) in der Vergangenheit	Geschichte in der Vergangenheit	Zeitindikator *when*
			a	

Present Perfect		
Nicht abgeschlossener Vorgang ohne Änderungen	Nicht abgeschlossener Vorgang in bestimmter Zeit	Vorgang mit noch sichtbaren Folgen

a) The small girl walked into the empty house and sat down at the breakfast table. She saw three bowls of hot porridge. She was very hungry.

b) Queen Elizabeth has been Queen of Britain for over 50 years.

c) The car has broken down. We must call the garage.

d) When my grandmother was young she worked on a farm.

e) There were no cars at the end of the last century.

f) France won the World Cup in 1998.

g) I've been in bed all day.

h) I didn't revise my vocabulary when I first learned English.

Welche Indikatoren gibt es, die uns daran erinnern, das *present perfect* zu benutzen?

Es gibt viele unterschiedliche Indikatoren, die das *present perfect* begleiten. Die meisten, aber bei weitem nicht alle, können in positiven und negativen Aussagen verwendet werden und natürlich auch in Fragen. Ihre Stellung im Satz verändert sich manchmal, je nach der Art des Satzes. An den folgenden Beispielen und Erklärungen siehst du, welches die richtige Position im Satz ist.

- Indikatoren, die sich auf Handlungen beziehen, die **bis zum Moment des Sprechens** abgelaufen sind und die ganze Zeit bis zu diesem Moment abdecken, sind z. B. *never, ever, up till now, all my life.*

Beispiele: I've never been to England
Have you ever smoked?
Up till now Meredith hasn't done very well in English but she's going to America in the summer and she hopes she'll be able to speak it better after that.
All my life I've wanted a horse and now my wish has come true.

Wenn du Fragen beantwortest oder Informationen erteilst zu Situationen, die diese Indikatoren beinhalten, dann musst du aufpassen: Die Fragen oder **allgemeinen Aussagen,** die du machst, beziehen sich auf dein Leben (oder das Leben von jemand anders) bis zum Moment des Sprechens, du verwendest also das *present perfect.* Sobald du aber **Einzelheiten** über **einen bestimmten, vergangenen Moment** in deinem Leben angibst, musst du die Zeitform wechseln und das *simple past* benutzen.

Beispiele: Bob: Have you ever seen a film by Stephen Spielberg?
Mary: Yes, I have. I saw *Stand by Me* when I was staying with my cousin in Newcastle-upon-Tyne.

- Indikatoren, die **Zeitspannen** zum Ausdruck bringen, die im Moment des Sprechens **noch nicht beendet sind,** wie z. B *today, this week, this month.*

Beispiele: No, you can't go out tonight. You've been out three times this week.
How many times have you been to the cinema this year?
I haven't eaten anything today because I don't feel well.

- ***just:*** Dies ist kein präziser Indikator. *just* zeigt an, dass wir uns in der Gegenwart befinden oder in der unmittelbaren Vergangenheit. Es wird mit „gerade" übersetzt.

Beispiel: I've just finished my homework (so I can come out with you).

- ***yet:*** *yet* kann mit „noch" oder „schon" übersetzt werden; ***not yet*** wird mit „noch nicht" übersetzt.

Beispiele: Have you phoned Mike yet?
I haven't phoned Mike yet.

- ***already:*** Der Sprecher geht davon aus, dass der Vorgang beendet ist, er dies aber nicht erwartete. Sehr häufig zeigt sich der Sprecher überrascht, weil das gegenwärtige Ergebnis sehr schnell zustande kam. *already* kann mit „schon" übersetzt werden. Benutze *already* **nur** in **verneinten Fragen**, aber nicht in verneinten Aussagen.

Beispiele: The baby has already gone to sleep. (Das ging diesmal aber schnell.)
Hasn't the train already left?
Have you already read this book?

- ***still:*** *still* wird im Allgemeinen in verneinten Sätzen benutzt und wird mit „immer noch nicht“ übersetzt.

  Beispiel: Hugh still hasn't fed the dog.
  (Warum ist der Hund in der Küche und schaut auf seiner leeren Napf?)

9. In the right place. Complete these sentences by putting the time marker in the correct position. Use the examples above and on the previous pages to help you.

a) He has gone to the dentist. (just) He has just gone to the dentist.

b) We've made the beds for you, mum. (already)

c) I haven't done it. (still)

d) Haven't you seen *Titanic*? (yet)

e) Has Mr Chapman marked our homework? (already)

f) Have you had a bath? (just)

g) They haven't decided what to do. (yet)

h) Hasn't she read it? (already)

10. Translation. Translate the above sentences – including the time markers – into German.

a)

b)

c)

d)

e) ____

f) ____

g) ____

h) ____

Wie bildest du die Formen des *simple past?*

Regelmäßige Verben bilden das *simple past* so:

- **Bejahte Form:** Hänge die Endung *-ed* in allen Personen, Singular und Plural, an den Infinitiv des Verbs.

  Beispiele: to walk → I walked
  to play → she played
  to remember → they remembered

- **Verneinte Form:** in der verneinten Form brauchst du die *simple past*-Form von *to do (did)* + *not* + Infinitiv des Vollverbs.

  Beispiele: to walk → I did not (didn't) walk
  to play → she did not (didn't) play
  to remember → they did not (didn't) remember

- **Frageform:** Wenn du eine Frage stellst, benutzt du *did* + Subjekt + Infinitiv des Vollverbs

  Beispiele: to walk → did I walk?
  to play → did she play?
  to remember → did they remember?

- Bei den meisten regelmäßigen Verben, die auf **-y** enden, musst du das *-y* zu *i* umformen, bevor du die *-ed*-Endung anhängst.

  Beispiel: to carry → carried

- Bei Verben, die auf ***-e*** enden, füge einfach *-d* hinzu.

Beispiele: to love → loved
to hate → hated

Es gibt auch einige **unregelmäßige Verben:**

- Diese sind nur als **bejahte Formen** unregelmäßig. Die Formen müssen gelernt werden. Als **verneinte** oder **Frageformen** folgen sie den gleichen Regeln wie die regelmäßigen Verben.

Beispiele:	to do	did	didn't do	did you do?
	to eat	ate	didn't eat	did you eat?
	to go	went	didn't go	did you go?
	to have	had	didn't have	did you have?
	to pay	paid	didn't pay	did you pay?

- ***to be*** ist vollständig unregelmäßig, weil es **weder** verneint **noch** als Frage ein **Hilfsverb** benötigt.

Beispiele:	I was	I wasn't	was I?
	you were	you weren't	were you?
	he was	he wasn't	was he?
	we were	we weren't	were we?
	they were	they weren't	were they?

Kurzantworten mit dem Hilfsverb:

- Wenn dir jemand eine Frage stellt, ist es unnötig, bei der Beantwortung das ganze Verb zu wiederholen. Du kannst dich in deiner Antwort auf das Hilfsverb beschränken. Du musst dabei immer die Zeit benutzen, die auch in der Frage auftaucht.

Beispiele: Did you go on holiday last year? ≈ No, we didn't.
Was the Battle of Hastings in 1068?
≈ No, it wasn't, it was in 1066.

Wie bildest du die Formen des *present perfect?*

- **Bejahte Form:** *present tense*-Form von *to have* + das Partizip des Vollverbs. Bei den **regelmäßigen Verben** stimmen das Partizip und das *simple past* überein. Bei den **unregelmäßigen Formen** sind sie meistens unterschiedlich.

Beispiele:	to walk	→	I have walked
	to be	→	we have been (unregelmäßig)

- **Verneinung:** *has/have + not*

Beispiele:	to walk	→	I haven't walked
	to like	→	he hasn't liked
	to think	→	she hasn't thought

- **Frage:** Um eine Frage zu bilden, vertausche Hilfsverb und Subjekt (Inversion).

Beispiele:	to walk	→	have I walked?
	to like	→	has he liked?
	to think	→	has she thought?

Kurzantworten mit dem Hilfsverb:

- Diese Regeln für alle Zeitformen sind die gleichen (s.o.).

Beispiele: Have you done the washing up yet, Charlie?
≈ No, I haven't. I'm going to do it in a minute.
Has your father mended your computer yet?
≈ Yes, he has. He did it last night.

11. Which is it? Complete the following short texts by filling the gaps with the correct form *(simple past* or *present perfect)* of the verbs in brackets.

a) Roald Dahl (die) ______________________________ in 1990. He (be) __________________ a famous writer and (write) ________________ for children and adults. Some of his books such as *Matilda, The Witches, Charlie and the Chocolate* Factory and *James and the Giant Peach* are very well known. Children all over the world (read) _______________ them.

b) The Channel Tunnel is not a new idea. Nicolas Desmerat, a French engineer, first (think) ________________ of a tunnel connection between Britain and France in 1750. However, there (be) ________________ many problems and it (take) ____________________ over 200 years before the French and British (agree) __________________ about the plans, money, etc. Work on today's Tunnel (start) ____________________ at the end of 1987. Today it carries many passengers between Britain and France but the British (still + not + accept) ____________________ it properly. For most people the English Channel and the ferries are still more popular.

c) BOB: (you + ever + hear) __________________________________ of the writer A. A. Milne?
MARY: Yes, of course I (auxiliary verb) ____________________. I (read) _____________________ quite a lot of his books. The last one I (read) __________________ was called *Winnie the Pooh.*
BOB: Oh, (you + know) ____________________ that Winnie the Pooh (be) _________________________ a real bear?
MARY: No, I (auxiliary verb + not) ______________________.
BOB: Well, her owner, a Canadian soldier from Winnipeg, (leave) ______________________ her at London Zoo in 1914. When she (arrive) _______________________ at the zoo Winnie, a black bear, (be) _____________ only a baby. Many children (visit) _____________ her and she (be) ____________ very friendly. One of the children who (visit) ____________ her (be) __________ Christopher Milne. When he (be) _____________ older he (write) _____________________ stories about her. The real Winnie (die) ___________________ in 1934 but because of Milne's stories noone (ever + forget) _________________________________ her really.

7.4 *present perfect progressive*

Wie das *present perfect* behandelt diese Zeitform Ereignisse, die in der **Vergangenheit** angefangen haben und noch mit der **Gegenwart in Verbindung** stehen. Die Verlaufsform hebt allerdings besonders hervor, dass diese Handlung **weiter anhält**, also noch nicht unterbrochen wurde, oder immer wieder **wiederholt wird.** Der betreffende Vorgang ist oft von **eingeschränkter Dauer.**

Rund um die Verwendung der Verlaufsform

Wann verwendest du das *present perfect progressive?*

- Du benutzt das *present perfect progressive,* um die **gegenwärtige Situation** oder das Erscheinungsbild des Sprechers zu erklären. Die **Folgen vergangener Handlungen** sind noch sichtbar. Die Handlung ist vielleicht gerade zu Ende gegangen oder der Sprecher hat diese für kurze Zeit unterbrochen und wird sie wahrscheinlich später wieder aufnehmen. Oft wird diese Zeitform auch benutzt, um sich zu **entschuldigen** oder um einen **Grund** für etwas anzugeben.

Beispiele: I must have a bath. I'<u>ve</u> <u>been</u> <u>running</u>.

(Ich bin gerade zurück gekommen, aber man kann die Folgen noch sehen: Ich bin heiß und schmutzig.)

I can't answer the phone – I'<u>ve</u> <u>been</u> <u>repairing</u> my bike.

(Ich repariere es immer noch und meine Hände sind ölig.)

I'm sorry I'm late. I'<u>ve</u> <u>been</u> <u>shopping</u> and it took a long time to get home.

- Während die *simple*-Form des *present perfect* vor allem das Ergebnis einer Handlung betont, stellst du mit der *progressive*-Form die **Tätigkeit an sich in den Mittelpunkt.**

Beispiele: I have cleaned the kitchen.
(Das Ergebnis wird betont: die Küche ist jetzt sauber.)
I have been cleaning the kitchen.
(Die Tätigkeit an sich wird betont. Du erzählst nur, wie du deine Zeit verbracht hast, ob die Küche schon sauber ist oder nicht, ist unerheblich.)

- **Ausnahme:** Wenn du davon sprichst, wie oft du eine Tätigkeit ausgeübt hast und eine genaue Zahl nennst, darfst du **nur** das *present perfect simple* verwenden.

Beispiele: I've been listening to my music all afternoon.
I've listened to 4 CDs already this afternoon.

Rund um die Form des *present perfect progressive*

Wie bildest du das *present perfect progressive*?

- **Bejahte Form:** present perfect von to be (has/have been) + present participle (-ing) des Vollverbs

Beispiele: I have been waiting for you.
She has been singing.

- **Verneinte Form:** *has/have + not + been + present participle* (*-ing*) des Vollverbs

Beispiele: I haven't been waiting long for you.
She hasn't been singing well this week because she's got a cold.

- **Frageform:** Vertausche das Subjekt und *has/have*

Beispiele: Have you been waiting long?
Who has she been singing with?

12. *Present perfect simple* or *progressive*? Complete the following sentences by selecting either the *simple* or *progressive form* of the *present perfect tense*.

a) Becky needs to wash her hair because she (paint) has been painting her room.

b) Zoe (never + read) ________________________ a book in her whole life!

c) Why are Beatrice's eyes so red?
≈ She (cry) ____________________ about George. He doesn't want to see her any more.

d) Two accidents (happen) ____________________ on the M25 motorway around London already today because people (drive) ________________ too fast in the foggy weather.

e) (you + wait) ________________________ a long time, Jimmy? You look freezing cold.

f) Carla (still + not + decide) ____________________________ what to do.

g) TOM: What's wrong, Matt?
MATT: Oh, nothing much. I'm just tired because I (work) ___________ __________________ late this whole week.

h) (Stuart + tell + yet) _________________________ you his exciting news ___________?

i) TRISH: Cameron (just + finish) ________________________ the book I lent him. Would you like to borrow it?
TINA: No, thanks, I (already + read) ___________________ it.

j) Morag (make) ______________________ cakes all day. It's her mother's birthday on Saturday and they (invite) __________________ 50 people!

Rund um die Verwendung von *for* und *since*

Wenn du die **Dauer** einer Handlung hervorheben willst, die noch nicht unterbrochen worden ist, dann kannst du das *present perfect progressive* zusammen mit einer Zeitangabe benutzen. Im Deutschen verwendest du „seit", um die Zeitangabe einzuführen. Im Englischen gibt es zwei Adverbien dafür: ***for*** und ***since.*** Schau dir folgende Tabelle an:

PAST	PRESENT
Your friend arrived at the tennis court at 2 o'clock.	It is now 3 p.m. and you have only just arrived at the tennis court.

Beispiele: Your friend says either:
I've been waiting for you since 2 o'clock or:
I've been waiting for you for an hour.

Je nachdem, ob du den **Zeitpunkt** angibst, seitdem du wartest oder die **Zeitdauer,** musst du ***since*** oder ***for*** verwenden. Die Zeitangabc (2 o'clock, an hour) ändert sich dann natürlich auch.

Wann benutzt du also *for*, wann *since*?

- ***for*** benutzt du in Ausdrücken, die auf den **Zeitraum** verweisen, in dem eine Handlung angefangen hat. Gebräuchliche Wörter sind in diesem Zusammenhang *an hour, years, a week, a long time, a moment* usw.
- ***since*** benutzt du in Ausdrücken, die auf einen **Zeitpunkt** verweisen, an dem eine Handlung anfing. Gebräuchliche Wörter sind *1 o'clock, last month, September, 1991* usw. Denke immer daran, dass dieser Zeitpunkt in der Vergangenheit liegt und ein Verb, das im Teilsatz mit *since* auftaucht, im *simple past,* nicht im *present perfect* stehen muss.

Beispiele: We've been learning English for two years.
We've been learning English since we started at secondary school in 1997.

past — **now**
1997 ——————→ 1999

since 1997 **for** 2 years

13. ***For* or *since?*** Complete the following table by putting these time markers under the correct heading in the table: *a month – I started school – a moment – the snow fell – my birthday – 2 weeks – 1987 – a long time – winter – last autumn – over 3 years – midnight –* ~~*about 20 minutes*~~ *– he was a small boy – a few years – the accident – three hours – a whole day*

for	**since**
about 20 minutes	

14. Practice makes perfect. Look at what all these people have been doing. Complete the following sentences with either *for* or *since.*

15. Altogether now please. Complete this text using either the *simple past, present perfect simple* or the *present perfect progressive*. With time markers you must decide whether to use *for* or *since*.

Cardiff (be born) ______________ about 2000 years ago when the Romans (build) ______________ a camp there. One thousand years later the Normans (make) ______________ the city much stronger with a medieval castle. Later still, in the 19th century, an important local man – the Marquess of Bute – (add) ______________ to the building: it (become) ______________ a comfortable place full of expensive furniture, beautiful pictures and lights and also wonderful wall decorations.

Cardiff Castle

Cardiff (be) ______________ a sea port and for many years – particularly during the 19th century – internationally important. Roald Dahl – the Norwegian writer – (be born) ______________ here in fact in 1916.
The city has got something for everybody – young and old. ______________ several years now children (enjoy) ______________ Techniquest – a very special sort of 'do-it-yourself'/'try-it-yourself' science museum. The National Gallery (become) ______________ the 'home' of some of Cézanne, Monet and Picasso's best paintings. Thousands of visitors come every year

to look at them. For music lovers there's something too, both classical and modern. Many international pop stars (play) ______________________ at St. David's Hall and ____________________ 1993 – when the Queen opened it – they (play) ____________________ at the Cardiff International Arena as well. For open air concerts, music lovers (always + go) ______________ ______________________ to Cardiff Arms Park where you can also watch international rugby matches. Rugby (always + be) ____________________ one of the most important kinds of sport in Wales.
Although Cardiff is a very old city it (only + have) _________________ the title of 'capital city' ____________________ 1955. But this is a modern city too. ______________________ a few years now the city's planners (build) ____________________ a 500 acre lake, an 8-mile waterfront and other buildings for businesses and leisure activities so that Cardiff will become one of Europe's most beautiful maritime cities.

16. Life line. You are on a school exchange visit to England. You find out lots of things about your 'exchange' and decide to write all this information down as a 'life line' so you can tell your family when you get back home. What questions did you ask to find out everything? In most of your questions and answers you will need to use either the *simple past* or the *present perfect*. Write the dialogue between you and your exchange using these words: *how many – when – how long – have you ever – how old*. You will also need to use the 'life line' on page 97 and the words in brackets to help you. Be careful of prepositions!

YOU: (to be born) When were you born?

EXCHANGE: ______________________________________

YOU: (to have got) ______________________________?

EXCHANGE: I've got two: one sister and one brother.

YOU: (to be born) ______________________________?

EXCHANGE: My sister ______________________ and my brother ______________________ 1991.

YOU: (to be) ______________________ when (to start) ________________ school?

EXCHANGE: ____________ five and a half. ______________________ September 1992.

YOU: (to learn + ever) __________________ a musical instrument?

EXCHANGE: Yes, ______________ – _______________ and ___________ but I (to not play) ____________________ the guitar anymore.

YOU: (to stop) __________________________________ ?

EXCHANGE: (to stop) ______________________________ January 1998.

YOU: (to play) ______________________________ the drums?

EXCHANGE: (to start) ____________________________ February 1998.

YOU: (to go on holiday + ever) ______________________________ ___________________________ to Germany?

EXCHANGE: Yes, __________. We ________________________________.

YOU: What sport do you like?

EXCHANGE: Judo.

YOU: Oh, how long (to do) _______________________________?

EXCHANGE: ____ 1994.

YOU: (to start) __________________________ secondary school?

EXCHANGE: (to start) ____.

YOU: Do you go to any clubs at school?

EXCHANGE: Yes, (to be) _____________ a member of ________________ ___________________________.

YOU: (to be) _________________________________ in the club?

EXCHANGE: (to be) ___________________________ since November 1997.

YOU: Have you always lived in this house?

EXCHANGE: ______________________________________.

YOU: (to move) __________________________________ here?

EXCHANGE: We (to move) _________________________ May 1998 so (live) here ____________________ for _____ years.

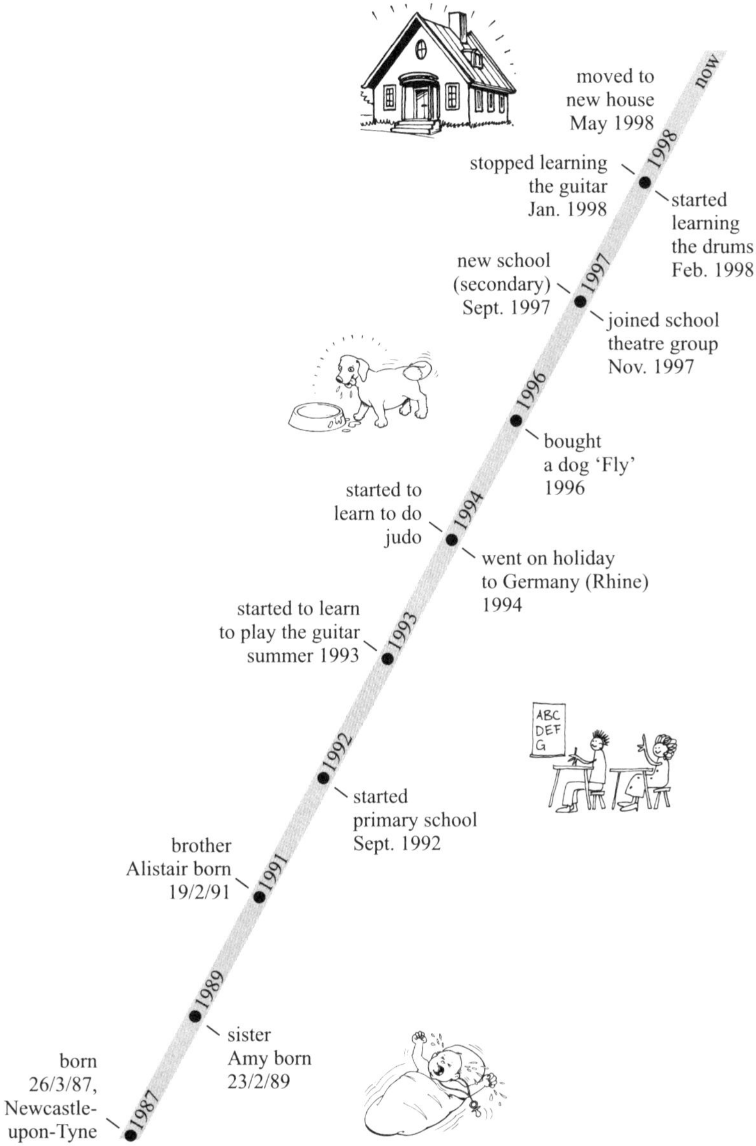
now
moved to new house May 1998
1998
stopped learning the guitar Jan. 1998
started learning the drums Feb. 1998
1997
new school (secondary) Sept. 1997
joined school theatre group Nov. 1997
1996
bought a dog 'Fly' 1996
1994
started to learn to do judo
went on holiday to Germany (Rhine) 1994
1993
started to learn to play the guitar summer 1993
ABC
DEF
G
1992
started primary school Sept. 1992
1991
brother Alistair born 19/2/91
1989
sister Amy born 23/2/89
1987
born 26/3/87, Newcastle-upon-Tyne

7.5 *past progressive*

Die meisten Zeitformen des Englischen sind Teil eines ‚Paares', d. h. dass es eine einfache *(simple)* Form und ein Verlaufsform *(progressive)* gibt. Beide Teile des ‚Paares' behandeln mehr oder weniger dieselbe Zeitform, aber sie betonen jeweils einen anderen **Aspekt.** Dies gilt auch für das *simple past.* Oft findest du *simple past* und *past progressive* auch zusammen in einem Satz.

Beispiel: When I got up it was snowing and the wind was blowing.

Wann benutzt du das *past progressive*?

- Du verwendest das *past progressive* bei Handlungen, die zu einem bestimmten Zeitpunkt in der Vergangenheit gerade **im Verlauf** waren.

  Beispiel: This day a month ago, we were enjoying our holiday in Spain.

- Das *past progressive* beschreibt eine **Rahmenhandlung:** während ein kürzer andauerndes Ereignis geschieht, läuft eine länger andauernde Handlung sozusagen im Hintergrund ab. Die **kürzere Handlung** wird im *simple past* wiedergegeben, die **Rahmenhandlung** im *past progressive.*

  Beispiel: A car came round the corner as I was crossing the road.
  (Der Sprecher war **gerade dabei**, die Straße zu überqueren. Er /Sie hatte schon angefangen, hatte aber die andere Straßenseite noch **nicht** erreicht.)

- Es kann dir vielleicht eine Hilfe sein, dir das *past progressive* als die Kulisse einer Bühne im Theater vorzustellen, also als etwas, dass für eine geraume Zeit unveränderlich bleibt. Im Gegensatz dazu kannst du dir die Schauspieler und Ereignisse, also ständig wechselnde Dinge, als das *simple past* verstellen.

  Beispiel: A car came round the corner as I was crossing the road. The car didn't see me and the driver braked too late. He hit me and I fell into the road. When I woke up I was in hospital.

- Das *past progressive* wird oft mit ***as*** oder ***while*** eingeleitet.

  Beispiel: While I was watching TV last night there was a thunderstorm.

Wie bildest du das *past progressive*?

Du benötigst für die *past progressive*-Form das *simple past* von *to be (was/were)* und das Partizip Präsens des Hauptverbs.

Beispiele: The cat was sleeping by the fire.
Were they singing loudly in church this morning?
I was sitting on my desk when a teacher came in.

17. Crossword. Complete the sentences with the correct form of the *past progressive*. Then complete the crossword with the *present participles* (from the *past progressive sentences)*. When you have completed the crossword you can answer the final question.

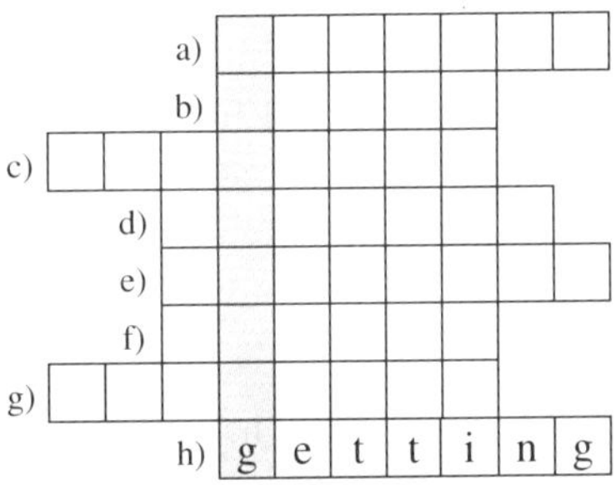

a) 

When I woke up this morning the sun ______________________.

b) 

Mum: Why (you) ____________________ in bed at 11.30 am yesterday Mary-Anne? It was such a beautiful day.

c) 

Danny cut himself on some glass on Sunday: his hand ____________________ badly.

d) 

Julia __________________ her new dress at my birthday party.

e) 

When the headmaster ___________________ to the pupils the alarm bell suddenly started to ring.

f) 

When I saw Marty yesterday he ____________ _____________ his new bike.

g) 

Milly and Johnny __________________ outside the bank when a man suddenly ran out with a gun in his hand.

h) 

The train started to leave the station when we were getting in.

What was Mary doing when her teacher Miss Peters asked her a question? She was ______________________.

Zusätzliche Regeln zum *past progressive*

- Wenn Ereignisse aus der Vergangenheit **nacheinander** passieren – in einer richtigen **Reihenfolge** – dann musst du das *simple past* für alle Verben benutzen und nicht zwischen *simple past* und *past progressive* unterscheiden. Vergleiche:

  Beispiele: I was waiting at the bus stop when the accident happened.
  (Als ich an der Bushaltestelle wartete, passierte der Unfall: Rahmenhandlung.)

  When the accident happened, I ran to the nearest telephone box.
  (Als der Unfall passierte, rannte ich zur nächsten Telefonzelle: nacheinander erfolgende Handlung.)

- Einige Verben **(statische Verben)** können **nicht** so ohne weiteres im *past progressive* benutzt werden (vgl. *present progressive* S. 71).

- Wie bei anderen Zeiten der Verlaufsform wird auch mit dem *past progressive* eine Handlung mit **beschränkter Dauer** beschrieben. Vergleiche:

  Beispiele: When I fed the horse he often bit me. (Es passierte jedes Mal.)
  When I was feeding the horse it bit me.
  (Es passierte nur dieses eine Mal.)

18. Over to you. Complete these sentences by using either the *past progressive* or the *simple past.*

a) Jackie's tooth (start) ________________________ to hurt as she (eat) ______________ her ice cream. Her mother (ring) ______________ the dentist the next morning.

b) The house (burn) _____________________ down when the man (fall) ______________ asleep with a cigarette in his mouth.

c) When the telephone (ring) ______________________, nobody (hear) ______________ it because Kim and Larissa (play) _____________ their music so loudly.

d) The door (open) _______________ slowly and a man in black clothes and a black hat (walk) _____________________ in. The children (be) ______________ very frightened.

e) When Carole (walk) ____________________ along the road she (slip) ______________ on a banana and (break) _______________ her arm.

f) My mother (clean) _______________ the windows and then she (cook) ______________ our lunch.

g) When Dave (walk) _________________ home from school he usually (visit) ________________ his grandmother.

h) As the robber (break) _________________ into the bank the alarm (go) ______________ off. The police (arrive) ________________ in a few moments and they (catch) _________________ him easily.

i) When we (travel) _________________ to Poland on holiday we (have) ____________ an accident. My whole family (have to) _____________ go to hospital. I (not enjoy) ______________ the holiday at all.

j) We (have) __________________ a good time in Cora's room when the neighbour (come) ________________ and (ask) _________________ us to turn the music down. He (say) _______________ he couldn't hear himself think!

19. The price is right. Fill the gaps in this story with the right form of either the *simple past* or the *past progressive.*

A man (walk) ____________________ down a street when he (suddenly + see) ________________ a 'For Sale' sign in the window of a nice red sports car. As he (look) __________________ at the car more carefully a woman (come) ___________________________ out of the house next to which the car (stand) _________________. She (ask) _______________ him, "Would you like to buy it? It's very cheap, only £10." The man (not + know) __________________ what to say: £10 (be) _____________ certainly very cheap. "There are more things in the house. Come in and look around", the woman said. He (follow) __________________ her into the house and while she (talk) _______________ to him and (show) ___________________ him all the things he (think) __________________ about everything. He (decide) ________________ to ask her why she (want) _______________ to sell the car, all the CDs and old records as well as two expensive tennis rackets so cheaply. The woman (look) _______________ at him for a moment and then she (say) ________________, "Well, it's a long story ..."

7.6 *past perfect*

Das *past perfect* (die Vorvergangenheit) benutzt du, wenn du von Handlungen und Zuständen sprichst, die sich **vor** einem bestimmten Zeitpunkt in der **Vergangenheit** ereignet haben.

Beispiel: When I got to school yesterday the lesson had already started.

Wann setzt du das *past perfect* ein?

- Das *past perfect* wird häufig zusammen mit dem *simple past* benutzt. Das *simple past* wird dabei als Indikator der Vergangenheit eingesetzt. Um anzuzeigen, dass die anderen Ereignisse, die beschrieben werden, noch **vor** dem vorher angezeigten Moment abliefen, musst du das *past perfect* verwenden.

  Beispiel: My mother got up at 7 o'clock and made my sandwiches for me. When I came downstairs at 7.30 the sandwiches were all ready.

  ⇓

  When I came downstairs at 7.30 my mother had made the sandwiches.

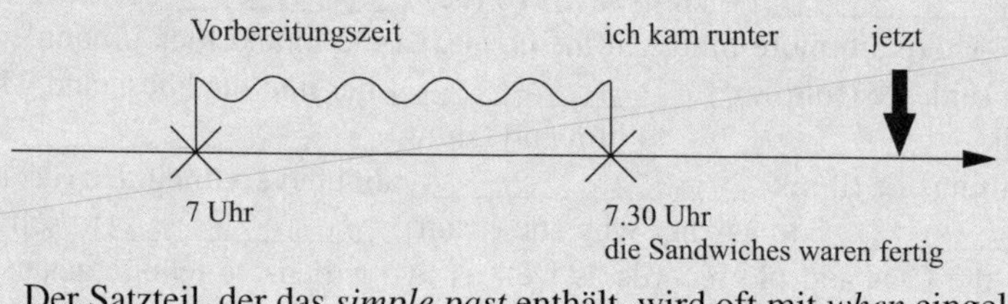

Der Satzteil, der das *simple past* enthält, wird oft mit *when* eingeleitet.

- Wird aber der Satzteil, der das *past perfect* enthält, als **Zeitindikator** benutzt, wird er mit ***after*** eingeleitet.

  Beispiel: We went to the cinema after we had done the shopping.

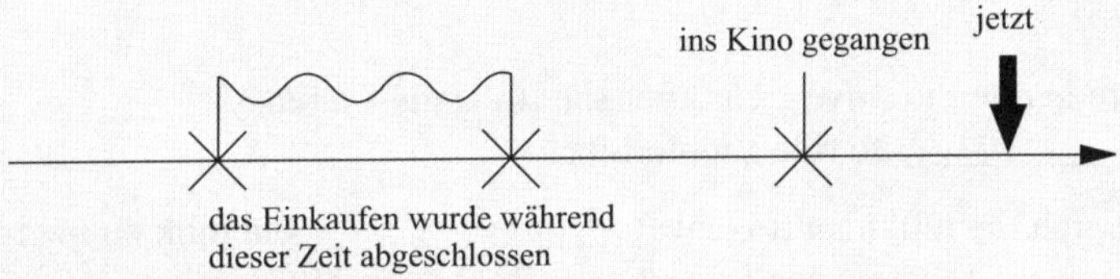

Wie bildest du das *past perfect*?

- **Aussageform**: simple past Form von to have (had) + past participle des Hauptverbs

  Beispiele: to walk → I had walked
  to play → you had played
  to think → he had thought

- **Verneinung:** Hänge *not* (Kurzform *n't)* an *had* an.

  Beispiele: I hadn't walked so far in all my life.
  She had not done her homework.

- **Frageform:** Vertausche *had* und das Subjekt.

  Beispiel: Had he thought he could really cycle to Edinburgh in five days?

20. Complete these sentences by putting the verbs in brackets in the past perfect

a) After we (to go) ___had gone___ to the swimming pool, we cycled home.

b) After our visitors (to leave) ____________________, we had to do a lot of washing up.

c) My brother (to repair + already) ____________________________ my CD player when I got home from school.

d) After Simon (to pass) _______________ all his exams, his parents bought him a new bike.

e) When Fabian stayed in England he went to an Indian restaurant. He (to eat + never) ____________________ curry in his life but he still liked it.

f) The description that Meredith (to give) ________________ to the police helped them to find the man who (to steal) ________________ her handbag.

g) Claire learned to drive a car after she (to learn + already) ____________ ______________ to ride a motorbike.

h) Although the milkman (to leave) _______________ the milk on the front step it wasn't there when I opened the front door this morning.

21. Linking. Join the following sentences to make one sentence. Sometimes you will need to use *because*. At least one of the verbs must be in the *past perfect!* Sometimes more than one answer is possible.

a) On Sunday morning Jerry got up at 11.45 a.m. His mother took the breakfast things off the table at 11.00 a.m.

When ____

____

Jerry ____

____

b) Cameron didn't do his French homework. The teacher made him stay longer at school.

____

____

____

____

c) Laura left her new jacket on the train. Her mother was very angry with her.

____

____

____

____

d) The party started at 8.30 p.m. Lauren arrived at 9.30 p.m.

____

____

____

____

e) Randall's nose bled badly. He had a fight with the class bully, Roger.

____

____

____

____

22. Visiting Guernsey. Lottie and Matt are on holiday with their parents in Guernsey. One day their parents decide to go to Herm, one of the other, smaller Channel Islands. Lottie and Matt don't want to go with them. Using the map, **mark in** where the children go and what they do. When you have done this, **join** the two sentences to make one using the *past perfect* and the *simple past*. (*Tip*: read the two sentences carefully and before you write anything decide which action happened first. This action should be written in the *past perfect.)*

a) Their parents give them £10 each to spend. Then their parents take the bus from Pleinmont Point, which is right near the holiday home, to St. Peter Port.

After their parents had given them £10 each to spend, they left and took the bus to St Peter Port.

b) First Lottie and Matt look at their map. They then decide to cycle to St. Andrew to look at the Little Chapel (which is the smallest church in the world and is made of shells and broken cups, plates, bowls, etc.).

____

____

c) They cycle along the road through Torteval and the Forest and then take the main road towards St. Andrew.

____

____

d) They go past the airport. They have to cycle for another 10 minutes and finally they arrive at the Little Chapel.

____

____

e) They eat an ice cream. After this they agree to go to the German Underground Military Hospital which is also in St. Andrew. (German soldiers built this hospital when they were living in Guernsey between 1940 and 1945.)

____

____

f) Lottie wants to visit the Moulin Huet Pottery because she wants to buy some souvenirs. They turn right at the crossroads in St. Andrew and take the road which goes down towards Moulin Huet Bay in St. Martin. It is a long way.

____

____

g) Before they eat their sandwiches and swim at the rocky beach there Lottie buys two big cups and a small mouse at the pottery.

____

____

h) They get back on their bikes. Then they cycle up the coast road right through the town centre of St. Peter Port until they get to Belle Greve Bay in St. Sampsons.

____

____

i) At Belle Greve Bay they turn left. They go towards Grande Havre Bay. They use the smaller roads because they are quicker.

____

____

j) They eat another ice cream and drink some cold water. Matt takes some photos of an interesting old French tower at Grande Havre Bay.

k) Because it is so hot they decide to go for a second swim. They cycle down to Vazon Bay, which is the sandiest beach in Guernsey and where it is fun to surf, and have a long swim.

l) By now it is almost 6 o'clock. They dry themselves and pack their rucksacks. They cycle back to their holiday home all along the coast road. Their parents are not yet there.

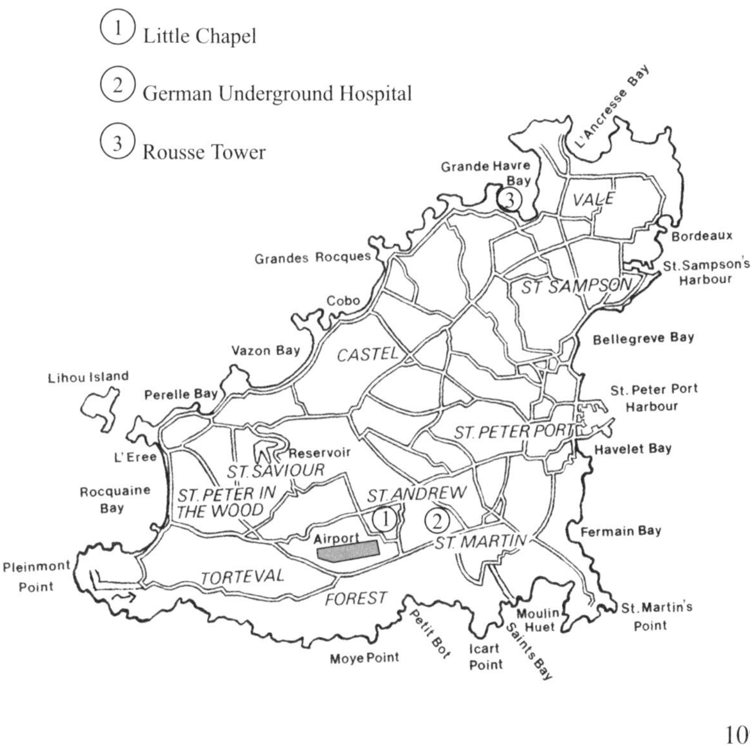

8 Modale Hilfsverben

Die modalen Hilfsverben *(modal auxiliaries)* halten sich nicht an die gewöhnlichen Vorgaben, die du Verben normalerweise zuschreibst: Sie haben ihren **eigenen Regelkatalog,** z. B. bezüglich der verschiedenen Zeitformen, und treten nicht als Vollverben auf. Du kannst mit den modalen Hilfsverben verschiedene **Sprechabsichten** ausdrücken:

- Ihre wichtigste Funktion besteht darin, aufzuzeigen, wie **wahrscheinlich, nötig, ratsam** oder **wünschenswert** die Handlung ist, die vom Vollverb ausgeht.
- Sie haben nicht nur eine Bedeutung, sondern mehrere, und diese **verschiedenen Bedeutungen** stehen in Verbindung miteinander.
- Die jeweilige Bedeutung wird durch den **Kontext, Betonung** und **Sprachrhythmus** beeinflusst

  Beispiele:

  You { can / needn't / mustn't / should / might } cycle to school.

Bevor wir uns die einzelnen modalen Hilfsverben etwas genauer anschauen, ist es ratsam, sich einige **allgemeine Punkte** vor Augen zu führen:

- Die modalen Hilfsverben weisen eine **Präsensform** und eine **Vergangenheitsform** auf, und zwar bei allen Personen. Allerdings stehen diese Formen nicht ganz streng in Verbindung mit dem, was man unter der wirklichen **‚Zeit'** von Gegenwart oder Vergangenheit versteht. Das Präsens kann auf eine gegenwärtige oder zukünftige Zeit verweisen; die Vergangenheitsform kann auf eine vergangene, gegenwärtige oder zukünftige Zeit verweisen. Vergleiche:

  Beispiele: My dog <u>can</u> do lots of tricks. (present tense, present time)
  You <u>can</u> go out tonight if you finish your homework.
  (present tense, future time)
  I <u>could</u> ride a horse when I was six. (past tense, past time)
  I <u>could</u> drive if you feel tired.
  (past tense, future time [near future or general future plan])
  That <u>could</u> be Sam's bicycle. Let me look. (past tense, present time)

- Einige modale Hilfsverben sind nicht vollständig in allen Zeitformen vertreten. Du musst in diesen Fällen **andere Verben** einsetzen. Diese sogenannten **Ersatzverben** treten in den verschiedenen Grammatiken immer zusammen mit den modalen Hilfsverben auf; sie sind aber **keine echten modalen Hilfsverben** und werden deshalb nicht in Anlehnung an die Regeln, die für die Modalverben gelten, gebildet, sondern nach den Regeln der Vollverben.

  Beispiele: <u>can</u> → <u>to be able to</u>
  <u>may</u> → <u>to be allowed to</u>
  <u>must</u> → <u>to have to</u>; Verneinung: <u>needn't</u> oder
  <u>not to be allowed to</u>

- Sie haben **kein Partizip Präsens** und können deshalb auch keine Verlaufsform bilden.

- Du kannst sie **nicht im Passiv** verwenden.

- Um eine **Frage** zu bilden, musst du das Subjekt und das Verb vertauschen. Du brauchst keine zusätzlichen Hilfsverben.

  Beispiele: Must we do it?
  Should we do it now or can we do it later?

- Die **Verneinung** bildest du, indem du *not* (Kurzform *n't*) an das modale Hilfsverb anfügst. Wenn du die bejahte Form eines Verbs verneinen willst, kann es vorkommen, dass du die **Bedeutung** des Verbs vollständig veränderst. Du musst demnach sehr aufpassen, wenn du Modalverben übersetzt.

  Beispiele: We must do our homework. (Wir müssen es tun.)
  We mustn't forget to do our homework. (wir dürfen es nicht tun.)
  We needn't do our homework today. (Wir brauchen es nicht tun.)

- Modale Hilfsverben bilden **keine Infinitivform:** Du musst auch hier ein anderes Verb verwenden, also wieder eine Ersatzform.

  Beispiele: I want to be able to leave at 7 o'clock tomorrow.
  (*can* kann hier nicht verwendet werden.)
  You're going to have to pack your bags tonight.
  (*must* kann hier nicht verwendet werden.)

8.1 *must*

Du kannst *must* mit „müssen“ übersetzen. Allerdings verändert sich die Bedeutung, sobald du *must* in der verneinten Form benutzt. Die unterschiedlichen Bedeutungen müssen gelernt werden. *must* existiert nur in der Form des *present tense.* Um die Vergangenheit und Zukunft auszudrücken, musst du das **Ersatzverb** *have to* verwenden.

- *must* hat im Deutschen drei Bedeutungen: **Zwang, Verpflichtung und Notwendigkeit.** Dabei musst du unterscheiden, woher der Zwang oder die Verpflichtung kommt: Wenn sie **vom Sprecher auferlegt** ist, benutzt du *must.* Wird die Verplichtung dagegen von einer **anderen Quelle** (Schule, offizielle Regeln) auferlegt, so musst du *have to* verwenden.

  Beispiele: I must write to my pen friend soon. I haven't written to him for a long time. (Zwang ist vom Sprecher auferlegt.)
  I have to stay late at school tomorrow because of the theatre group. (Der Zwang kommt von außen.)

- In der Aussageform bezieht sich *must* ausschließlich auf **gegenwärtige und zukünftige Situationen.** In allen anderen Zeiten musst du es durch *have to* ersetzen.

  Beispiele: We must go now. (present tense, present time)
  I must clean my bicycle on Saturday. It's so dirty. (present tense, future time)
  I had to go to the dentist yesterday. (past tense, past time)
  My grandfather has never had to go to hospital. (present perfect)

- Wenn du **Fragen** oder **Verneinungen** im *simple present* oder im *simple past* bildest, benötigst du das Hilfsverb *do + (not) + have to.*

  Beispiele: Emma doesn't have to go on holiday with her parents this year because she's going on a special riding holiday in Wales.
  Why do you have to leave so early?
  When the circus came to our village the children who are still at primary school didn't have to pay.
  What did Matt have to do when he went to see the headmaster?

	Zwang kommt vom **Sprecher;** Ausdruck einer persönlichen Meinung	**Zwang** kommt von **anderer Quelle;** Darstellung von Fakten
Welches Verb wähle ich?	***must*** (müssen) *I must go now.* (Ich muss jetzt gehen.)	***to have to*** (müssen) *You have to wear a helmet when you ride a motorbike.* (Man muss einen Helm tragen, wenn man Motorrad fährt.)
Wie verändert sich die Bedeutung in der Verneinung?	**Zwang → Notwendigkeit** (nicht [zu tun] brauchen)	**Zwang → Erlaubnis** (nicht [tun] dürfen)
Ersatzformen	*do not have to (don't have to)* *need not (needn't)* *You don't have to/needn't go now.* (Du brauchst jetzt nicht zu gehen.)	*must not (mustn't)* *to be not allowed to* *You mustn't/aren't allowed to ride a motorbike without a helmet.* (Ohne Helm darf man nicht Motorrad fahren.)

1. **Getting it right.** Complete the following sentences with either *must* or the correct form of *to have to*. Sometimes both are possible.

   a) It's 10.30. I really must/have to go.

   b) Because Sally did badly in her test, she ________________ do it again.

   c) British children ___________________ wear school uniform.

   d) My dad has got a new job and we are moving house. I _______________ change schools too.

e) I ______________________ telephone my grandmother tonight. It's her birthday.

f) John ______________________ go to the dentist last Monday because his tooth was hurting badly.

g) Shirin's parents have got a shop. Sometimes she ___________________ help there when it's very busy.

h) Your bus leaves in 10 minutes. You ___________________ leave now if you don't want to miss it.

i) Sorry I'm late Miss Hutchins. I __________________ go to the doctor's this morning.

j) I saw a very good film last week at the cinema. If it comes to your town, you _______________ go and see it.

2. Questions. Fill the gaps with the correct form of *to have to* and finish the sentence. Use personal pronouns *(you, she, he,* etc.) where possible in the question to make the question sound like natural English.

a) I have to go.
Why *do you have to go?*

b) British schoolchildren have to do their homework in the evening.
Why ____

c) Colin had to see the headmaster.
When ____

d) Jack and Jill will have to do more work if they want to pass the English test.
Why ____

e) We have had to buy a lot of new books for school.
How ____

f) Kathy has to get up early tomorrow.
What time ____

g) Angus has had to help at home a lot this week.
Why ____

3. Negatives. Fill in the gaps with the correct negative form of *to have to*.

a) Do I have to come with you, Mum to visit Auntie Norah? I've got so much to do.
≈ No, Mel, you don't have to come with me but please do all your homework before you go out with your friends.

b) Did you pay for the bike yourself?
≈ No, I ______________________________ because my grandparents bought it for me.

c) Daniela doesn't do much work for English. Is she lazy?
≈ No, she ______________________________ because her mother is American. She's so lucky.

d) Do you walk to school?
≈ No, I go to a boarding school so I ______________________: I live in it!

e) What will you do if the weather is bad tomorrow? It's not possible to have a barbecue party in the rain.
≈ I ______________________ anything because my mother said we're going to have it in the garage if the weather is so bad.

f) Lisa, get up, you're late for school. It's after half past eight.
≈ Mum, don't worry! We ______________________ go to school today: Mr Dibble is ill and he won't be back until Monday. I'm sure I told you last night.

4. More negatives. In this exercise put either *mustn't/don't have to* or *doesn't have to* in the gap to complete the sentences.

a) You ______________ drive fast in towns, cities or villages because it's dangerous.

b) If your hands are wet, you ______________ touch electricity.

c) Some children ______________ help their parents at home ever.

d) We ______________ go to bed early tonight because tomorrow is the first day of the school holidays.

e) Sonja ______________ eat sugar. If she does, she gets very ill.

f) Has anyone ever told you a secret? You ________________ ever tell it to anybody else.

g) After you have cleaned your teeth at night you ________________ eat anything.

h) In Germany pupils ________________ wear school uniform.

i) When you go to Britain you ________________ take any animals with you.

j) You ________________ come to the meeting but I think you'll find it very interesting.

k) Anna ________________ buy any clothes because her mother makes them all for her.

Andere Alternativformen zu *mustn't* und *don't have to*

- *don't have to* ist die verneinte Form (hinsichtlich seiner Bedeutung) von *must*. Ein weiteres Verb, dass du hier einsetzen kannst, ist *needn't* (= ‚es ist unnötig'). *needn't* hat **keine Vergangenheitsform.** Du darfst *needn't* (modales Hilfsverb) **nicht** mit der verneinten Form des gewöhnlichen Vollverbs *to need (to)* **verwechseln.** Dieses kann ganz normal in allen einfachen Zeiten durchkonjugiert werden (allerdings nicht in den Verlaufsformen!). Anstelle von *needn't* kannst du also auch *doesn't/don't need to* benutzen. Vergleiche:

Beispiele: I <u>don't</u> <u>have to</u>/<u>needn't</u>/<u>do not need</u> <u>to</u> do this now.
(*present tense:* alle drei Alternativen sind möglich.)
You <u>didn't</u> <u>need to</u> leave early. (*need* als Vollverb)
Sibyl <u>hasn't</u> <u>needed to</u> wear glasses for a long time.
(*need* als Vollverb)
You <u>won't</u> <u>need to</u> write the letter. (*need* als Vollverb)
In the end they <u>hadn't</u> <u>needed</u> the extra money their parents had given them. (*need* als Vollverb)

- *mustn't* kannst du im Deutschen mit „nicht dürfen" übersetzen. Eine Alternative für *mustn't* ist ***not to be allowed to.*** Da dies ein gewöhnliches Verb ist, kannst du es in allen Zeiten konjugieren.

  Beispiele: Joanna isn't allowed to/mustn't stay out late.
  Women in Britain weren't allowed to vote until 1928.
  We won't be allowed to go in if we are too late.
  The Smarts haven't been allowed to build a swimming pool in their garden.

5. Translation into English: Meine Mutter ging auf ein Internat für Mädchen. Sie mussten sich an viele strenge Regeln halten:

- Du darfst auf dem Flur nicht rennen.
- Du musst aufstehen und „Guten Morgen" oder „Guten Tag" sagen, sobald ein Lehrer ins Klassenzimmer kommt.
- Du darfst die Schule während der Woche nicht verlassen.
- Du musst dein Zimmer aufräumen und die Bettwäsche einmal pro Woche wechseln.
- Du musst das Licht um 20.30 ausmachen.
- Wenn das Licht aus ist, darfst du nicht reden oder Musik hören.

Ein Vergleich zwischen *needn't, must* und *mustn't*

- *must:* Es ist **wichtig**, etwas zu tun.

  Beispiel: The train leaves in 8 minutes. We must hurry.

- *mustn't:* Es ist **wichtig**, dass man etwas **nicht tut.**

  Beispiel: If you want, you can tell Jason but you mustn't tell anybody else.

- *needn't:* Es ist **nicht wichtig**, das man etwas tut.

  Beispiel: The train only leaves in an hour. You needn't hurry.

6. **Dos and don'ts.** A friend of yours is going to stay with a Scottish family. You've been to Britain before and can give your friend a few useful tips about how life is different. Complete the sentences using *mustn't, needn't* or *must.*

a) 

You ________________ drive on the right.

b) 

You ______________ carry an ID card.

c) 

You ____________ wear a school uniform.

d) 

You ____________________ get up so early for school.

e) 

You _________________ say your surname when you answer the telephone.

f) 

You ____________ go to school in the afternoon every day.

g) 

Most British policemen ______________ carry a gun.

7. Saying it in a different way. Re-write these sentences: *needn't → doesn't/don't need to; doesn't/don't need to → needn't*

a) When you are 16 you needn't go to school any more.
When you're 16 you don't need to go to school any more.

b) In Britain many people think they needn't clean their cars every Saturday. In Germany it's different!

____

____

c) Although the weather in Britain can be bad you don't need to believe everything that you hear. It isn't always foggy and it doesn't always rain.

____

____

d) Visitors to Britain needn't worry about the food: it's much better than most people say it is!

____

e) In Britain you don't need to keep quiet on Sundays. Lots of shops are open and you are allowed to make as much noise in your house and garden as you like!

____

____

8.2 *can/may* und andere Ersatzformen

Wann verwendest du *can* und *to be able to?*

- *can* und *to be able to* besagen beide, dass etwas **möglich** ist, oder dass jemand die **Fähigkeit** besitzt, etwas zu tun.

  Beispiele: You can play the piano very well.
  Can Charlie help you? I'm busy at the moment.

- *can* ist ein echtes modales Hilfsverb; es hat eine Form für die Gegenwart *(simple present: can)* und für die Vergangenheit *(simple past: could).* In allen anderen Fällen benutzen wir allerdings die **Ersatzform** *to be able to.*

  Beispiele: Madonna can dance very well. (present tense)
  She could dance when she was five. (past tense)
  Sarah hasn't been able to do sport for a long time because she broke her leg when she was skiing. (present perfect)
  I think I'll be able to repair my bicycle. (future)
  You must be able to do it. (infinitive)

- Obwohl *can* und *could* immer von *to be able to* ersetzt werden können, werden in der Regel *can* und *could* eingesetzt, wenn diese Formen an der jeweiligen Stelle möglich sind. *could* wird insbesondere mit den folgenden Verben benutzt: Verben der Sinneswahrnehmung *(see, feel, hear, taste, smell), understand* und *remember* und mit Verben, die eine allgemeine Fähigkeit einer Person zum Ausdruck bringen.

  Beispiele: I could smell something delicious. (Sinneswahrnehmung)
  Could you understand what I was saying?
  Could you remember what happened at the end of the film.
  Steffi Graf could play tennis when she was only three.
  (allgemeine Fähigkeit)

- Um die **Verneinung** zu bilden, musst du *not* nach *can* oder der passenden Form von *to be* einfügen.

  Beispiele: Skyler can't swim very well.
  They weren't able to find the CD you asked for.

- Um die **Frageform** zu bilden, vertausche einfach *can* (oder *to be)* und das Subjekt.

  Beispiele: Can you speak French?
  Could you understand the film? I found it a little difficult.
  Was Maddy able to go with you to the concert?

8. Choices. Decide whether to complete the following sentences with the correct form of *can*, *could* or *be able* to. Sometimes more than one is possible. Be careful with tenses!

a) When I was eight I (not) couldn't/wasn't able to swim.

b) ______________ you drive already?
≈ No, I __________, but I'm going to have lessons when I'm 17.

c) Simon hasn't __________________ find the book you wanted to borrow from him.

d) Josh had a very bad cold last week and he (not) ________________ smell, taste or hear anything.

e) I haven't _________________ do my homework yet because none of the lights in our house work and I (not) ______________ see anything.

f) Last week I tried to watch a film in English but I (not) ________________ understand very much at all. It was so fast.

g) Why doesn't Terry answer. He must __________________________ hear me.
≈ Oh, I ____________ see why he (not) __________________ hear you: he's listening to his walkman.

Welche modalen Hilfsverben brauchst du, um Forderungen zu stellen, Erlaubnis zu geben oder ein Angebot zu machen?

Wenn du **freundlich nach etwas fragen** willst, kannst du drei verschiedene modale Hilfsverben verwenden: *may, could* und *can.* Manchmal spielt es keine Rolle, welches Hilfsverb du einsetzt, in anderen Fällen kann nur ein besonderes benutzt werden.

Beispiele:

May / Could / Can } I have the ketchup, please?

Can / Could } you please be quiet?

Can I help you at all, sir?

- Um **nach etwas zu fragen**, kannst du *may I ...? /could I ...? /can I ...?* benutzen. Sie unterscheiden sich lediglich durch die Situation, in der sie gebraucht werden. Dabei ist das eine etwas förmlicher, das andere weniger förmlich. *may* wird außerdem im Allgemeinen nur in **Fragen in der Kombination mit *I* oder *we*** benutzt und kommt in **Fragen nie mit *you*** vor.

wenig förmlich →	**neutral** →	**sehr förmlich**
unter Freunden; ältere Person zu jüngerer Person	in allen Situationen	im Umgang mit Leuten, bei denen es sehr auf Höflichkeit ankommt
can I ...?	*could I ...?*	*may I ...?*
(darf ich ...?)	(dürfte ich ...?)	(dürfte ich ...?)

Beispiele: Oh Ann, can you please open the door for me? My hands are full.
Excuse me, could you tell me the time, please?
Do you think you could lend me £1.50? I'll give it back to you tomorrow.
May I have that watch please? The red one at the back on the left.

- Um **nach Erlaubnis zu fragen,** ob du etwas tun darfst, kannst du ebenfalls entweder *may, could* oder *can* einsetzen (beachte bitte die verschiedenen Stufen der Förmlichkeit).

Beispiele: Hello, this is Melissa. Can I speak to David, please?
Could you spell your name again please, Sir? I didn't hear it properly.
May I close the window, please. It's rather cold in here.

- Um jemanden **Erlaubnis zu erteilen**, kannst du nur *can* oder *may* benutzen.

Beispiel: You can (may) go to the football match but please be careful.

- In bestimmten Situationen kannst du *can* benutzen, um jemanden **etwas anzubieten.**

Beispiel: Can I help you? You look a little lost.

In welchen Situationen kannst du *to be allowed to* einsetzen?

to be allowed to ist ein normales Vollverb. Du benutzt es, um eine **Erlaubnis einzuholen** oder auch **zu erteilen**. Es hat somit mehrere Funktionen:

- Es kann alle fehlenden Formen von *may/may not/mustn't* ersetzen: Diese modalen Hilfsverben gibt es nur im Präsens.
- *may* und *may not* werden nur in **Fragen** und **Antworten** benutzt. In allen anderen Fällen musst du *to be allowed to* benutzen. *not to be allowed to* ist die **verneinte Form** und kann *mustn't* (= nicht dürfen) ersetzen.

Beispiele:
Luke: May I stay at the party until midnight, Dad?
Dad: Yes, you may but make sure you don't miss the last bus.
Sam: And me, Dad? What about me?
Dad: No, you may not go Sam. You know you're not allowed to stay out after 10.30.
Sam: That's not fair. Luke is always allowed to stay out late.
Dad: When I was your age we were only allowed to stay out until 9 o'clock.

9. Situations – Getting it Right. Complete the following sentences using the correct form of *can, could, may* or *to be allowed to*. Don't forget the subject pronoun either!

a)

"My name is Dwight Witherspoon. I'd like to speak to Frank Smith."
"Sorry, Mr er, er ____________________ say your name again, please?"

b)

__________________ have some more please, mum? It tastes so good.

c)

Oh, Mrs Carpenter. _____________ carry your bags for you? They look very heavy.

d)

Waiter, ______________ have the bill, please?

e)

__________________ borrow your car tonight, please, dad? I've looked at the bus timetable and the last one leaves at a quarter to ten.

8.3 *shall* und *will*

- Wenn du jemandem deine **Hilfe anbieten** möchtest, dann kannst du entweder *can I ...?* (siehe S. 126) oder *shall I ...?* einsetzen. Du kannst *shall I ...?* (Plural: *shall we ...?*) auch benutzen, um einen **Vorschlag zu machen** oder um **nach Rat zu fragen.**

  Beispiele: Shall I cook supper tonight, mum? We learned how to make something in our cookery lesson and I want to try it out.
  (= Do you want me to cook ...?)

  Shall I meet you at 7.30 tonight after youth club?
  (= I suggest ... What do you think of my suggestion?)

  Where shall we go on holiday this year? (= Where do you suggest?)

  I like the shoes a lot but they're a bit expensive. Shall I buy them or not? (= What advice can you give me?)

- Wenn du jemanden fragen möchtest, **etwas für dich zu tun**, dann kannst du entweder *could you ...?* oder *can you ...?* benutzen. Oft kannst du aber auch *will you ...?* verwenden. *will you ...?* hat aber viel mehr als *could* und *can* den Charakter einer **Aufforderung.**

  Beispiele: Will you turn the music down, please. It's much too loud.
  (Machst du bitte ...?)

  Will you pass me the potatoes, Val. They're too far away.
  (Reichst du mir bitte ...?)

  Will you please stop talking?
  (Sei /Seid bitte ruhig.)

10. Questions. Fill in the gaps using either *will you*, *shall I* or *shall we* as necessary.

a) 

Where ______________________ go? To the swimming pool or down to the football ground?

b) 

_______________ get them or not?

c) 

Megan, _______________ please tidy up your room N O W !!!

d) 

What _____________________ get Kate for her birthday? Have you got any good ideas what I could buy? She's got so much already.

e) 

What time ___________________ meet you this evening, Andy? Is 6.30 OK?

f) 

Zoe, _____________________ please clean the blackboard? Mart is ill today.

11. Situations. Read the situations and then write a sentence using *shall I ...?*

a) You're going to London for the day and you don't know how much money to take. You ask your mother:
Shall I take £15 or £20?

b) It's freezing cold and the window is still open in the classroom. You speak to your teacher:
______________________________, Miss Deane?

c) You shouted at your boyfriend because he said he wanted to go out with his friends on Saturday and not with you. You want to ring him up and say sorry. Ask your friend for advice:
Sarah, ______________________________ or not?

d) You're shopping with a friend. You see some CDs you like but you're not sure which one to get. Ask your friend for advice:
Which ____________________, Dave? The new one by *98°* or this one by *B*witched*?

Now write sentences with *shall we ...?*

e) You and your friend haven't decided where to go out on Saturday. You ask:
Where shall we go out on Saturday?

f) You're in London with a friend. You want to go to Oxford Street. You don't know if it's better to go by tube or by bus.
______________________________ or by bus?

g) Your class is planning a birthday surprise for your teacher, Mr Linklater. You're not sure if it's OK to decorate the classroom or not. Ask the others in your class what they think.
____

8.4 *should* und *ought to*

- Möchtest du jemandem einen **Rat geben**, jemanden an seine **Pflichten** erinnern oder **warnen**, dann musst du *should* oder *ought to* benutzen. (*ought to* ist das einzige modale Hilfsverb, das mit der Präposition *to* auftritt). Beide Wörter haben die **gleiche Bedeutung.** Übersetzte *ought to* und *should* mit „sollte" oder „sollte eigentlich".

  Beispiel: You should (ought to) go to the dentist.

- Willst du diese Formen **verneinen,** dann füge einfach *not* an

  Beispiel: People shouldn't (ought not to) drive if they are feeling tired.

- In manchen Fällen hat *should (ought to)* eine ähnliche Bedeutung wie *must. must* ist allerdings stärker.

  Beispiele: You should do more sport.
  (Es wäre eine gute Idee, aber du musst es nicht unbedingt tun.)

  You must do more sport.
  (Es ist wichtig und unbedingt nötig, z. B. aus gesundheitlichen Gründen, dass du mehr Sport machst.)

12. Positive or negative? Fill in the gaps using *ought to (should)* or *shouldn't (oughtn't to)* as necessary.

a) You ________________ go to bed earlier.

b) You ________________ go to bed with wet hair.

c) I don't think you ________________ do that. It's dangerous.

d) I ________________ get up earlier. Then I could be on time for school!

e) Our neighbours really ____________________ keep their dog inside the house at night. It's always barking.

f) You ________________ always have lights on your bike at night.

13. **Necessary or not?** Complete these sentences using *must* or *should/ought to*.

a) When the lights are red you ____________________ stop immediately.

b) On a motorcycle you ______________________ wear a helmet.

c) When you go on holiday to a place you don't know you ______________ buy a guide book and a map.

d) When you buy something in a shop you _____________ pay for it.

e) I think Pete ____________________ get a little more pocket money.

f) Many people think you _____________________ always sleep with the bedroom window open.

* **14.** **Saying it differently.** Re-write the following sentences with a different modal. Make sure the meaning doesn't change. In this exercise you will need to use **all the modals** you have learned about.

a) When you buy petrol you aren't allowed to smoke.
When you buy petrol you mustn't smoke.

b) Was it necessary for you to buy such a big dog?
____

c) Children under ten are allowed to come in free.
____ pay anything.

d) Can I go to bed a little later tonight? There's a good film on.
____

e) In an exam you aren't allowed to talk.
____

f) In most British schools children have to wear a tie.
____

g) In some families boys don't have to help around the house at all.
____

h) May I borrow £3 from you, mum, please till Saturday?
____

8.5 Konjugationstabellen

must, needn't + alternative forms (müssen, nicht brauchen/nicht müssen)

	Aussageform	Verneinung
present tense	I *must* pay I *have to* pay --- (ich muss bezahlen)	--- I *don't have to* pay I *needn't* pay (ich brauche nicht zu bezahlen)
past	I *had to* pay (ich musste bezahlen)	I *didn't have to* pay (ich brauchte nicht zu bezahlen)
present tense	I *have had to* pay (ich habe bezahlen müssen)	I *haven't had* to pay
will-future	I *will have to* pay (ich werde bezahlen müssen)	I *won't have to* pay (ich werde nicht bezahlen müssen)

can, can't + alternative forms (können, nicht können)

	Aussageform	Verneinung
present tense	he *can* sing he *is able to* sing (er kann singen)	he *can't* sing he *is not able to* sing (er kann nicht singen)
past	he *could* sing he *was able to* sing (er konnte singen)	he *couldn't* sing he *wasn't able to* sing (er konnte nicht singen)
present perfect	he *has been able to* sing	he *hasn't been able to* sing
will-future	he *will be able to* sing (er wird singen können)	he *won't be able to* sing (er wird nicht singen können)

can, may, mustn't + alternatives (dürfen, nicht dürfen)

	Aussageform	Verneinung
present tense	they *can* go they *may* go they*'re allowed to* go (sie dürfen gehen)	they *mustn't* go they *may not* go they *aren't allowed to* go (sie dürfen nicht gehen)
past	they *were allowed to* go (sie durften gehen)	they *weren't allowed to* go (sie durften nicht gehen)
present perfect	they *have been allowed to* go (sie haben gehen dürfen)	they *haven't been allowed to* go (sie haben nicht gehen dürfen)
will-future	they*'ll be allowed to* go (sie werden gehen dürfen)	they *won't be allowed to* go (sie werden nicht gehen dürfen)

should/ought to (sollen)

	Aussageform	Verneinung
present tense	you *should* come you *ought to* come (du solltest kommen) (Sie sollten kommen)	you *shouldn't* come you *ought not to* come you *oughtn't to* come (du solltest nicht kommen) (Sie sollten nicht kommen)
past	---	---
present perfect	you *should have* come you *ought to have* come (du hättest kommen sollen) (Sie hätten kommen sollen)	you *shouldn't have* come you *ought not to have* come (du hättest nicht kommen sollen) (Sie hätten nicht kommen sollen)
will-future	---	---

9 Passiv

Wir benutzen das Passiv *(passive voice)* immer dann, wenn wir die **Handlung an sich** herausstellen möchten oder wenn wir der von der **Handlung betroffenen Person/dem Gegenstand** besondere Aufmerksamkeit zuteil kommen lassen möchten. **Wer** die Handlung ausgeführt hat, **interessiert uns dann nicht, wissen wir nicht** oder **ist unerheblich.** Vergleiche:

Beispiele: The thief stole an expensive picture from the National Gallery in London. (Der Handelnde *the thief* wird hervorgehoben.)

An expensive picture was stolen from the National Gallery in London.
(Der Schwerpunkt ist verschoben: der Gegenstand, um den es geht, wird betont: *an expensive picture.)*

Im Passivsatz wird also das **Objekt des Aktivsatzes** (hier: *expensive picture)* zum **Subjekt!** Das Subjekt des Aktivsatzes (hier: *the thief)* fällt im Passivsatz entweder weg oder wird als *by-agent* genannt *(An expensive picture was stolen by the thief.).*

Wie bildest du das Passiv?

Alle Zeiten im Aktiv können auch im Passiv ausgedrückt werden. Du musst nur die richtige Form von *to be* einsetzen. Stelle dir immer folgende zwei Fragen bei der Bildung des Passivs:

- Steht das Objekt des ursprünglichen Aktivsatzes im Singular oder im Plural?
- In welcher Zeitform steht das Verb im ursprünglichen Aktivsatz?

Sobald du diese beiden Fragen korrekt beantwortet hast, kannst du alles, egal in welcher Zeitform, im Passiv sagen und schreiben.

- Wenn das Objekt ein Pronomen ist, wird es im Passiv zum Subjektpronomen.

Objektpronomen	→	**Subjektpronomen**
me	→	I
you	→	you
him	→	he
her	→	she
it	→	it
us	→	we
them	→	they

- ***simple present*:** *am/is/are + past participle* (Partizip Perfekt) des Vollverbs

Beispiele: (S: People; V: speak; O: French, Italian and German)

People speak French, Italian and German in Switzerland.

Objekt steht im Plural, also steht im Passiv ***are.***

Partizip Perfekt des Vollverbs *speak*, also steht im Passiv ***spoken.***

French, Italian and German <u>are</u> <u>spoken</u> in Switzerland.

(S: People; V: call; O: me)

People never call me Jeremiah, they always call me Jem.

Objekt steht im Singular *(me)*, also steht im Passiv ***I + am.***

Partizip Perfekt des Vollverbs *call*, also steht im Passiv ***called.***

I'<u>m</u> never <u>called</u> Jeremiah, I'<u>m</u> always <u>called</u> Jem.

- ***simple past*:** *was/were + past participle* des Vollverbs

Beispiele: (S: Englishmen; V: built; O: the new castle at Aberystwyth)

Englishmen built the new castle at Aberystwyth between 1277 and 1279.

Objekt steht im Singular *(the new castle)*, also steht im Passiv ***was.***

Partizip Perfekt des Vollverbs *build,* also steht im Passiv ***built.***

The new castle at Aberystwyth <u>was</u> <u>built</u> between 1277 and 1279.

- ***present perfect:*** *has/have + been + past participle* des Vollverbs

Beispiel: Somebody has taken my purse. (Aktiv)
My purse has been taken. (Passiv)

- ***will-future:*** *will + be + past participle* des Vollverbs

Beispiel: Somebody will steal that if you leave it there. (Aktiv)
That will be stolen if you leave it there. (Passiv)

1. **The late farmer.** Below is a timetable of what Farmer Brown has to do every day. Yesterday he woke up an hour later than usual. Write sentences using the *simple past* in the *passive voice* about what happened **yesterday**.

a) Yesterday the pigs were fed at eight o'clock.

b) ______

c) ______

d) ______

e) ______

f) ______

g) ______

h) ______

i) ______

2. **Sold.** Mr and Mrs Bangert want to sell their house but nobody wants to buy it because they haven't looked after it very well. Finally a young man and his wife say they'll buy the house but Mr and Mrs Bangert must do a few things first. Look at picture A and then write down what the young couple say needs to be done. Use the will-future passive.

A

B

a) The fire-place in the living-room will have to be taken away.

b) The roof (to mend) ______

c) Some flowers (to plant) ______

d) The grass (to cut) ______

e) The fence (to paint) ______

Three months later the young couple come back. Mr and Mrs Bangert have not finished everything. Compare pictures A and B and write down what the young couple say. Use the *present perfect passive + still + not.*

f) The grass still hasn't been cut.

g) The door (to paint) ____________________

h) The windows (to clean) ____________________

i) The rubbish (to take away) ____________________

Was musst du noch über das Passiv wissen?

- Nicht jeder Aktivsatz kann ins Passiv verwandelt werden. Es gibt kein Passiv bei Aktivsätzen mit **Verben, die kein Objekt haben** (es gibt keinen Satzteil, der zum Subjekt werden könnte), wie z.B. *to arrive, come, cry, die, fall, go, laugh and smile.*

  Beispiel: The lesson starts at 9 o'clock.

- Falls du den Handelnden im Passivsatz auch erwähnen willst, dann musst du ihn mit der Präposition ***by*** einführen. Die handelnde Person des Aktivsatzes ist nicht mehr länger das Subjekt des Passivsatzes. Er wird zum *by-agent*.

  Beispiel: At 6 o'clock the farmer feeds the pigs.
  At 6 o'clock the pigs are fed by the farmer.

- Das Passiv wird vor allem in Zeitungsartikeln, bei technischen Beschreibungen und historischen Darstellungen angewandt (also da, wo die beschriebenen Dinge am wichtigsten sind).

  Beispiele: The gardens at Hever Castle were created between 1904–1908.
  Water is cooled in this machine here.

- **phrasal verbs** können auch im Passiv benutzt werden. **Trenne** aber **nie** die Präposition vom Verb.

  Beispiel: An au-pair looks after the children when I go to work.
  The children are looked after by an au–pair when I go to work.

- **Modale Hilfsverben** können ebenso im Passiv stehen. Im Aktivsatz folgt dem Modalverb ein Infinitiv. Im Passivsatz sieht dies genauso aus: Modalverb + Infinitiv von *to be + past participle* (= Infinitiv im Passiv.) Diese Form des Infinitivs im Passiv benutzt du, um Empfehlungen auszusprechen oder um Regeln zu erklären.
  Die **verneinte Form** bildest du, indem du *not* vor *to be* einfügst. Du bildest **Fragen**, indem du das Subjekt (des Passivsatzes) und das Modalverb umstellst (Inversion).

  Beispiele: You must leave the hot water on.
  (Subjekt + modales Hilfsverb + Infinitiv des Vollverbs)
  The hot water must be left on.
  (Subjekt + modales Hilfsverb + Infinitiv im Passiv: to be + past participle)

3. Rules. Complete these rules using the passive infinitive of these modals: *have to; should* or *ought to; must/mustn't.*

a) Uniforms (wear) have to be worn every day at this school.

b) Teeth (clean) ______________________________ three times a day. Not everybody does it.

c) Most animals (feed) __________________________ in the morning and evening.

d) Helmets (wear) ___________________________ at all times.

e) Sign in hotel: Baths (take) ______________________ after 10 p.m.

4. **Who does what?** Match the pictures of the people with the names of their jobs. Now match the people up with the one thing which they need in their job and the correct verb. Then make a passive sentence with the *by-agent*.

a)		a nurse	do	
b)		a magician	repair	
c)		a doctor	do	
d)		a mechanic	take	
e)		a teacher	steal	
f)		a thief	type	
g)		a chef	correct	
h)		a milkman	cook	
i)		a secretary	deliver	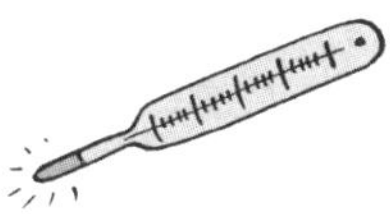

a) Cars are repaired by a mechanic.

b) ______________________________

c) ______________________________

d) ______________________________

e) ______________________________

f) ______________________________

g) ______________________________

h) ______________________________

i) ______________________________

5. **Famous lives and events.** What did these people do and what happened in these places? Find out and then complete these sentences using the passive voice. You will need to include *by* + the 'doer'. Add any other prepositions which are necessary too.

a) *We are the Champions* – to sing – the band – *Queen.*
We are the Champions was sung by the band Queen.

b) *Robinson Crusoe* and *Moll Flanders* – to write – Daniel Defoe.
____

c) The French and Napoleon – to beat – the battle of Waterloo – the Duke of Wellington.
____

d) The Conservative Party – to lead – Margaret Thatcher – 1975–1990.
____

e) Oxygen – to discover – Carl Wilhelm Scheele and Joseph Priestly – 1777.
____

f) The *Mona Lisa* - to paint – Leonardo da Vinci.
____

g) London – to destroy – the Great Fire – 1666.

____

h) The atomic bomb – to use – Japan - the United States – the first time – 6 August 1945.

____

6. Historical Wales. Complete this text about a place in Wales which receives thousands of visitors every year. Use the passive voice.

© Cadw Welsh Historic Monuments

Tintern Abbey lies not far over the border into Wales between Chepstow and Monmouth. The abbey is a mediaeval monastery which (to set up) __________________ for Cistercian monks on 9 May 1131 by an Anglo-Norman, Lord Walter Fitzrichard de Clare. At the beginning the monks did not have much land but over the years land (to give) ______________ to them. All the work in the fields and woods, etc. (to do) _______________ by the monks themselves and other people who worked for the monks – very simple men who wanted to work for the church. Later – in the 15th century – cottages and shops (to add) ________________ to the Abbey – but outside the walls.
When Henry VIII (to make) _________________ king in 1509 life for religious people – monks, nuns, priests – changed seriously. Because he wanted to control the Church, about 800 places of catholic religion (to close) ______________ between 1536 and 1540 and (to give) ______________ to the king, including Tintern, on 3 September 1536. The Anglican church

(to start) _______________ by Henry VIII when he broke away from Rome in 1534. All the silver, pictures, etc from the abbey (to send) ____________ _______________ to the king. The roof, which (to make) _______________ of lead, was valuable. In 1541 it (take off) _________________ and melted. Even the windows (to break) _________________________ and (to destroy) ____________________.

Tintern was lucky – it still exists today – but others do not: all the building stones (to take away) _______________ and (to use) _______________ for other buildings. In 1756 work (to begin) ___________________ to save the abbey: rubbish (to remove) _____________________, the ground (to make) _______________ flat and grass (to plant) ________________ .
Several paintings (to do) _______________ of the abbey by the well-known English artist JMW Turner between 1792 and 1798. The poem *Lines composed a few Miles above Tintern Abbey* (to write) ________________ by the famous poet William Wordsworth in 1798. In 1901 the abbey (to buy) __________________ by the state and since 1914 it has been the property of Cadw-Welsh Historic Monuments.

10 Gerundium

Das Gerundium *(gerund)* ist eine **infinite Verbform,** d.h., es gibt genau wie der Infinitiv und das Partizip keine Angaben zu Person, Numerus und Zeitform des Verbs. Das Gerundium besitzt sowohl Eigenschaften des Nomens als auch des Verbs und ist somit eine Mischform, die verschiedene Funktionen im Satz einnehmen kann. Als **nominales Verb** kann es im Satz wie ein Nomen eingesetzt werden. Es kann also sowohl Subjekt als auch Objekt eines Satzes sein oder durch eine Präposition eingeführt werden. Das Gerundium hat immer die **Endung *-ing*.**

Beispiele: Cycling is my favourite sport. (Subjekt)
Some people hate lying in the sun. (Objekt)
I'm interested in finding out more. (nach Präposition)

Das Gerundium als Subjekt

- Da sich das *gerund* z.T. wie ein Nomen verhält, kann es das **Subjekt** eines Satzes sein. Es gibt im alltäglichen Leben etliche **Schilder** und ähnliche Hinweise, die das *gerund* auf diese Weise einsetzen.

  Beispiele: Dancing is easy.
  No smoking

- Da das Gerundium auch Elemente des Verbs aufweist, kann es ein **Objekt** oder eine **Adverbialphrase** nach sich haben (Adverb der Zeit bzw. des Ortes).

  Beispiele: Doing sport makes you healthy. (Objekt)
  Working in the holidays is terrible. (Adverb der Zeit)
  Going to the cinema every week is very expensive.
  (Adverb des Ortes und der Zeit)

1. My hobby. What do these people say about their hobbies? Re-write these sentences using a gerund construction. Use the word in brackets ( ) and the underlined words to help you.

a) I think chess is a great game. (play)
Playing chess is great.

b) I go to the swimming pool every day. It's a hobby of mine. (favourite)
____

c) I do a lot of sport, especially athletics, at school. I can run very fast and I usually win. (best)
____

d) I often go to the mountains at the weekends with my father to climb. (dangerous)
____

Now try *without* the underlined words to help you.

e) I never go to the disco because I can't dance. (difficult)
____

f) I sing in a choir at my church. Some people think it's a strange hobby but I don't. (not stupid)
____

g) Some children watch a lot of TV. I don't know why – I've got better things to do. (boring)
____

2. Signs and instructions. What do these signs and instructions tell you not to do?

a)  ____________________

b) 

c) 

Das Gerundium als Objekt

Nach bestimmten Verben – insbesondere nach solchen, die über Gefühle sprechen (positive und negative) – musst du ein *gerund* benutzen. In diesen Fällen ist das Gerundium Objekt des Satzes. Verben, die oft ein Gerundium fordern, sind z. B. *like, love, enjoy, hate, can't stand, don't like.*

Beispiele:	**Subjekt**	**Verb**	**Gerundium**
	I	love	playing tennis.
	Hazel	can't stand	washing the dishes.

3. Likes and dislikes. Look at these activities and decide what you feel about them (see the verb scale at the side): some you love, others you only like and others you even hate! Sort them out concerning your feelings. Then make two sentences for each 'feeling' using the gerund construction.

100 %	LOVE	go out with my friends
		tidy up my room
		sing
		do the washing up
		listen to music
	ENJOY	help in the garden
		look after my little brother/sister
		play tennis
		lay the table
	LIKE	sew my own clothes
		try new recipes
		swim
		read science fiction stories
		do maths
	DON'T LIKE	look after my pet
		read fan magazines
		get up early
		play the piano, the guitar, the drums, etc
		go on holiday with my family
	CAN'T STAND	eat chocolate
		sleep
		buy clothes
		work on the computer
		go to the cinema
		talk to my friends
0 %	HATE	mend things

Example: I don't like getting up early.

a) ____________________

____

b) ____________________

____

c) ____

____

d) ____

____

e) ____

____

f) ____

____

Das Gerundium nach Adjektiv und Präposition

Einige Adjektive haben immer eine ganz bestimmte Präposition bei sich. Sie werden zusammen mit *to be + gerund* verwendet. Du darfst die Präposition nicht vom Adjektiv trennen.

Beispiele:	**Subject**	**Verb**	**Gerund**
	I'm	(not) interested in	learning new things.
	I'm	(not) good at	mending things.
	I'm	tired of	waiting for my friend.

Aufgepasst: die Präpositionen sind im Deutschen unterschiedlich:

to be interested in	sich interessieren für
to be good at	gut sein in
to be tired of	leid sein etw. zu tun

4. **What are these people good at?** Look at the pictures and then write a sentence for each person.

a) 

He's good at taking photos.

b) 

____

c) 
____

d) 

____

5. **Analysis.** What sort of *gerund* is in each of these sentences? Put the answer in the table. Be careful: two of the sentences have got a normal *-ing* form *(present continuous)!* Which ones?

Gerund as subject	*Gerund as object*	*Gerund after adjective + preposition*
a		

The two 'trick' sentences are ________ and ________.

a) Waking up is hard to do.

b) Some people are very good at saving money. I'm not.

c) The French love taking a long time to eat their food.

d) I could never be a model: I can't stand wearing lovely clothes all the time. I like my jeans much better.

e) I'm listening to my music at the moment so you'll have to go to your bedroom if you want to listen to yours.

f) Working from 9–5 is very British. People say, "I've got a nine-to-five job."

g) We can't leave yet because Rhiannon is still having a bath. I don't know how much longer she wants to stay in there.

h) Aren't you interested in finding out who the murderer in the book was?

6. Translating into English. Be careful with the gerund constructions!

a) Findest du, dass das Sammeln von Teddybären ein interessantes Hobby ist?

____

b) Wie hieß denn dieser Schauspieler damals, der auch so gut tanzen konnte? ≈ Meinst du Fred Astaire? Ja, den meine ich!

____

____

c) Warum hast du kein Interesse daran, mitzukommen?

____

d) Immer wenn ich viel Geld habe, gehe ich sehr gerne einkaufen.

____

e) Ich finde Angeln langweilig, aber viele Leute finden es interessant.

____

f) Meine Aufgabe zu Hause ist es, mit dem Hund spazierenzugehen.

____

g) Ich hasse es, Horrorfilme anzuschauen, wenn ich alleine bin. Und du?

____

11 Bedingungssätze

Wenn du Bedingungssätze *(conditional sentences)* benutzt, dann sprichst du über Situationen oder Begebenheiten, die nicht unbedingt Gestalt annehmen: der Sprecher stellt sich das Ergebnis einer bestimmten Situation (der Bedingung) nur vor. Der **Bedingungssatz** besteht immer aus **zwei Teilen:** aus dem ***if*-Satz** (der Bedingung) und dem **Hauptsatz** *(main clause)*. Der Inhalt des Hauptsatzes hängt dabei vom *if*-Satz ab. Wird die Bedingung nicht erfüllt, kann oder wird das Ereignis des Hauptsatzes nicht vonstatten gehen.

Beispiele: If we go to Scotland this year, we'll go to the Isle of Skye.
If we went now, we would be on time.

Bedingungssätze sind ein wenig wie ein kompletter Satz von Dominosteinen, die alle in einer Reihe aufgestellt werden. Wenn du dann den ersten anstößt, fallen alle anderen auch um. Es wird sozusagen eine Kettenreaktion ausgelöst.

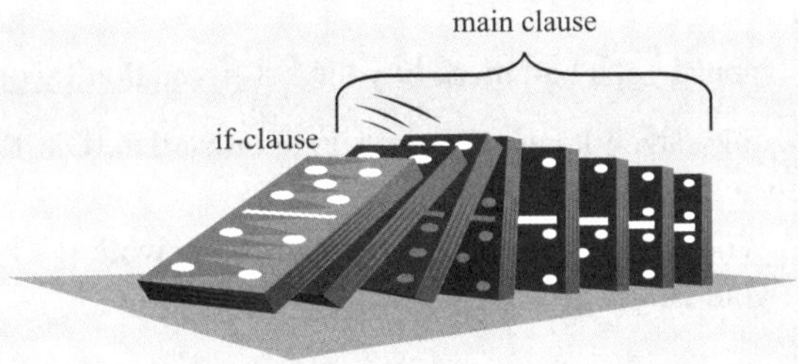

11.1 Bedingungssatz Typ I *(Conditional I)*

- In diesem Satztyp wird eine **erfüllbare Bedingung** ausgesprochen. Der Sprecher macht Voraussagungen hinsichtlich der **Zukunft.** Er ist sich seiner Meinung über das, was passieren kann, **ziemlich sicher.** Trifft die Bedingung des *if*-Satzes (A) tatsächlich ein, wird der Inhalt des Hauptsatzes *(main clause)* [B]) mit Sicherheit auch eintreffen. Trifft die Bedingung von A allerdings nicht ein, dann kann es auch nicht zu B kommen. In diesem ersten Typus der Bedingungssätze **kann** die Bedingung **erfüllt werden.** Die zwei Hälften des *Conditional I*-Satzes weisen jeweils eine unterschiedliche Zeitform auf:
  if-Satz: *simple present,* Hauptsatz: *will-future*

Beispiel:	**A: *if*-Satz**	**B: Hauptsatz *(main clause)***
	If you eat healthily,	you'll grow up big and strong.
	(if + simple present,)	*(+ will-future)*

- Die Stellung des *if*-Satzes nimmt keinen Einfluss auf die Bedeutung des Satzes. Er kann am Satzanfang stehen oder auch nach dem Hauptsatz. Steht der *if*-Satz wirklich nach dem Hauptsatz, dann musst du das Komma weglassen.

  Beispiel: You'll get a bad mark in your test if you don't work hard.

- Mit Bedingungssätzen kannst du auch **Fragen** stellen. Die Konjugationsregeln bleiben dabei unverändert.

  Beispiel: Will you help me with my maths homework if I help you with your English?

1. Matching. Complete these sentences by finding the correct other half.

a) If the sun is hot,	we'll be first.
b) If I save enough money,	the river will flood.
c) If I leave now,	we'll call it Emily.
d) If you lose your new jacket,	we won't be able to go on holiday this year.
e) If you invite Rob to your party,	many people will be unemployed.
f) If my mother loses her job,	you will get brown.
g) If the factory closes,	I'll buy myself the new Celine Dion CD.
h) If it rains any more,	I'll be very angry.
i) If the team wins today,	I won't come.
j) If it's a girl,	I'll be able to catch the 10.48 train to Penzance.

2. Another country. Patel is Indian. He has recently moved to a new school in Bradford. One day, he finds a letter in his desk. It is not very nice. It says: *Foreigners go home.* He shows it to his teacher. The teacher decides to talk to the class. She asks them a question. *If we send all the foreigners home, what will happen to Britain?* Look at the example and then write more sentences in the same way:

Italy	If	we won't have any pizza.
India		curry.
France	the French	much/many
Japan		so many
China		
Switzerland		
Germany		

Der Gebrauch von modalen Hilfsverben in Bedingungssätzen

Modale Hilfsverben können ganz unproblematisch in beiden Teilen eines Bedingungssatzes verwendet werden. Benutzt du *can, may, must* im Hauptsatz, dann **verändern sie die Bedeutung des Satzes.** Vergleiche:

- ***may***

Beispiele:

A: *if*-Satz	**B: *main clause***
If I've got time,	I'll mend it for you.

(B wird mit Sicherheit erfüllt werden, wenn A eintritt.)

If I come by bike,	I may not be there before it's dark.

(Hier kann man nicht ganz sicher sein, dass B eintritt, selbst wenn A erfüllt wird.)

If you do your homework now,	you may go to Chris's house after tea.

(Der Sprecher benutzt *may*, um eine **Erlaubnis** zu erteilen. A muss zuerst erfüllt werden.)

- ***must/mustn't***

Beispiele:

If you go to Edinburgh,	you must visit the castle.

(Der Sprecher erteilt einen **Rat** oder **befielt** etwas.)

If you go to the swimming pool,	you mustn't swim in the deep end.

(Hier **verbietet** der Sprecher etwas.)

- ***can***

Beispiele:

If you leave now,	you will get there on time.

(Man wird sicher pünktlich sein.)

If you leave now,	you can get there in time.

(Der Sprecher hebt hervor, dass man durchaus noch die **Möglichkeit** hat, pünktlich zu sein.)

If you help me,	you can/can't go.

(Hier spricht der Redner davon, ob er eine **Erlaubnis erteilt** oder **nicht.**)

3. Which modal auxiliary? Fill the gaps using *can/can't*; *may/may not*; *must/ mustn't*. Sometimes more than one answer is possible.

a) If we buy a dog, Mum says we may/can have a sheepdog like Lassie.

b) If you go up Ben Nevis, you __________ go where it is very dangerous.

c) If you go to Canterbury, you ______________ visit the Canterbury Tales museum. It's really very interesting and the guide also speaks German!

d) If you go to see that film, they __________ let you go in. You don't look 18.

e) You ____________ have the main part in the school play if you promise to work hard.

f) If you don't tidy up your room soon, you __________ have your pocket money for this week.

g) We ___________ go through this field if the farmer's bull is there. He'll run after us.

h) Of course you ____________ understand the game if you don't read the rules first.

Der Gebrauch von Imperativen mit dem Bedingungssatz des Typs I

Du kannst auch **Imperative** (Befehlsformen) im Hauptsatz einsetzen. Der Sprecher teilt einer Person mit, was **gemacht werden soll.** Dies hängt natürlich auch weiterhin davon ab, ob A eintrifft. Vergleiche:

Beispiele: If you get up before me, please make breakfast.
(Der Sprecher ordnert etwas an: Indem er *please* einfügt, bleibt es höflich und nicht zu offensichtlich.)

If you get up before me, will you please make breakfast?
(Hier stellt der Sprecher eine höfliche Forderung in Form einer Frage.)

If I get up before you, I'll make breakfast.
(Der Sprecher erwähnt einfach nur Tatsachen, er stellt keine Forderungen.)

4. What's possible? Complete these sentences using either the standard tenses for conditional I *(simple present/will-future),* an imperative or a modal auxiliary.

a) If it snows tonight, I (build) will/may/can a snowman tomorrow: I love snowmen.

b) If you (send) ___________ the letter today, Granny (get) _________ it by Friday but if you (do) ______________ it any later, it (not + arrive) ____________________ in time for her birthday.

c) I know this old car (not start) ______________ in the morning if I (not + leave) _______________ it in the garage tonight.

d) If I (find) ___________ your key, I (tell) _________ you. Don't worry!

e) I know I (have to) _________ go to the dentist's if I (eat) __________ too many sweets.

f) Please (buy) _________ some stamps for me if you (have) _________ time.

g) If the match only (start) ____________ at three, we (to be) _________ there in time. Don't panic!

h) I'm sure the cake (be) ______________ ready before we need to leave if you (put) ____________ it in the oven now.

11.2 Bedingungssatz Typ II *(Conditional II)*

- Auch dieser Bedingungssatz bezieht sich auf die **Zukunft.** Allerdings handelt es sich beim *conditional II* um eine **Bedingung,** die **voraussichtlich nicht eintreten wird.** Der Sprecher glaubt nicht, dass die Bedingung A erfüllt werden kann oder wird: Die erwähnte Situation wird **wahrscheinlich** nicht eintreten. Die zwei Hälften des *Conditional II*-Satzes weisen jeweils eine unterschiedliche Zeitform auf:
  if-Satz: *simple past, main clause: would + infinitive (conditional II)*

Beispiel:	**A: *if*-Satz**	**B: *main clause***
	If I did well in my English test,	my teacher would be very surprised.
	(*If + simple past,*	*would + infinitive* of main verb)

- die Vergangenheitsformen der **modalen Hilfsverben** können eingesetzt werden, um die Bedeutung des Hauptsatzes B zu ändern: *may → might; can → could.*

  Beispiel: If we left earlier, we {might} get there on time.
  {could}

- Das *conditional II* setzt du auch ein, wenn du über **Träume und Pläne** redest, oder darüber, wie du eine bestehende Situation verändern würdest, wenn du könntest; also immer dann, wenn du dabei bist, dir eine Situation vorzustellen. Dies ist dann eine **unwirkliche aktuelle Situation**, die du weder kontrollieren noch ändern kannst, die dich aber immer wieder zum Nachdenken anregt.

  Beispiel: Situation: you want to send a birthday card to your friend Charlie but you don't know the date.
  You say: "If I knew the date, I would send Charlie a birthday card."

- Anders als im Deutschen, darfst du ***would* (oder *will*) nicht in den if-Satz** (Bedingungssatz) einbauen, sondern **nur im Hauptsatz.** Dieser kleine Merksatz soll dir helfen, daran zu denken:

If and would is not good.

Vergleich: *conditional I* versus *conditional II*

Wieso musst du beide Formen der Bedingungssätze lernen? Beide drehen sich doch um die Zukunft!

Es gibt allerdings erhebliche **Bedeutungsunterschiede.** In beiden Fällen hat der Sprecher schon ein gewisses Vorwissen über **Situation A** und kann deshalb einschätzen, ob das Ereignis durchaus **eintreten kann** *(conditional I)* oder aller Voraussicht **nicht ablaufen** wird *(conditional II).* Vergleiche:

Beispiele: If we go to America next year, we'll visit my aunt in Washington.

(Wir gehen nächstes Jahr mit Sicherheit in Urlaub, wissen aber noch nicht wohin [ob nach Amerika oder irgendwoanders].)

If we went to America next year, we would visit my aunt in Washington.

(Ich bin mir nicht sicher, ob **a)** wir nächstes Jahr überhaupt in Urlaub gehen oder **b)** jemand von meiner Familie überhaupt nach Amerika gehen will oder **c)** wir genügend Geld für solch eine Reise haben oder **d)** andere Gründe, nicht nach Amerika zu fahren.)

5. Situations. Re-write these sentences with *if* + conditional II.

a) This soup is too salty. It doesn't taste nice.
This soup would taste nice if it was less/wasn't so salty.

b) I'm not going to buy that book because it's too expensive.
If that book ______

c) I'd like to go on holiday in Britain but the weather isn't always good.
If the weather ______

d) I would like to lend you some money but I'm afraid I haven't got any.
I ______

e) I can't go to the cinema with you because I have to look after my little brother.
If I ______

f) We can't have a barbecue because it's too cold.
If it ______

6. Possible/unlikely? Read these situations and then decide which sentence fits it better. Put a ✓ in this box. Remember: the condition is only in the *if-clause*.

a) It's early October:	"If it snows tomorrow, I'll be surprised."	☐
	"If it snowed tomorrow, I'd be surprised."	☑
b) Lindsay Davenport:	"If I win at Wimbledon this year, I'll be very happy."	☐
	"If I won at Wimbledon this year, I'd be very happy."	☐
c) fashionable girl:	"If I change my hair colour, my mother may be angry."	☐
	"If I changed my hair colour, my mother might be angry."	☐
d) very good pupil:	"If I do badly in the test next week, I'll be angry with myself."	☐
	"If I did badly in the test next week, I'd be angry with myself."	☐
e) small boy:	"If I have lots of money, I'll buy myself a new football."	☐
	"If I had lots of money, I'd buy myself a new football."	☐
f) It's summer:	"If the sun shines tomorrow, we can go swimming."	☐
	"If the sun shone tomorrow, we could go swimming."	☐

✷ **7. Quiz.** Read each situation and then tick (✓) the sentence ending which best answers what you think you would do (if you were in this situation). When you have finished the quiz, write a conditional II sentence for each situation with a tick. Remember to change pronouns *(you → I)*, etc. Be careful of tenses.

What would you do if ...?

1. Your history teacher gives you two weeks to finish a project. You think
   a) "No problem. I've got lots of time."
   b) "That deadline isn't fair."
   c) "I won't be able to finish in time. Help!" ✓

   If my history teacher gave me two weeks to finish a project, I would think ... "I won't be able to finish in time. Help!"

2. Your mother says you've got to tidy up your room before you are allowed to go shopping. You
   a) push everything under the bed.
   b) don't know where to start because it's so untidy.
   c) start straight away and plan to do it properly. You'll be finished in about an hour or so.

   ________________ I had got to tidy up my room before I was allowed to

   ____

3. You want to get a part-time job so you can buy some new clothes, CDs, shoes, etc. You
   a) dream all day about the 'perfect' job but don't try to find one.
   b) decide after half an hour that you don't want to have a boss – or anybody else (parents, teachers or sports coach) – who has to tell you what to do.
   c) suddenly see you're too busy to have a job.

   ____

   ____

4. You promise your best friend to help get everything ready for his/her party but at 7 p.m. you are
   a) still in your room because you can't decide what to wear.
   b) on the way to the house but you are walking slowly because your friend always asks you to help and you've had enough.
   c) still in the supermarket because you can't decide what sort of food to buy.

   ______________________________ for his/her party, at 7 o'clock I ______________________________

   ____

5. Your friend asks you to go to the cinema with him/her. The film starts at 8 p.m. You
   a) arrive late but you have a good excuse.
   b) may arrive late if you don't think the film is very interesting.
   c) arrive early and keep good seats for both of you.

   ______________________________ with him (her) and the film started at 8 o'clock, I ______________________________

6. You aren't very interested in your boy/girlfriend any more. You
   a) wait for him/her to say 'goodbye': somebody is better than nobody. You look for someone else at the same time.
   b) several times 'forget' to meet him/her at your meeting place: you hope he/she will soon understand why.
   c) tell him/her straight away. You're too honest and you think it's only fair to tell the truth.

   ____

   ____

7. You get ketchup on your favourite pair of white trousers. You
   a) wash the trousers straight away.
   b) throw them in the back of the cupboard and only find them when you're looking for a shoe.
   c) hide them with the other washing and hope your mum doesn't notice.

   ____

   ____

8. Your teacher gives you a test but you don't understand the instructions. You
   a) wait for someone else to ask.
   b) say nothing because you don't want anyone to think you're stupid.
   c) say nothing because you know the teacher has made the test extra hard and that she/he won't help you anyway.

   ____

   ____

8. Mixed conditionals. The Mallett family – Mum, Dad and the twins Anne and Jamie – are planning their summer holidays. Complete the text using the correct form of either *conditional I* or *conditional II.*

MUM: I think we should go to north Wales first. It's so beautiful and there are lots of mountains.

DAD: Yes, that's a good idea. Let's do that. If we (start) ____________ in the north, we (can + drive) ________________ down to mid Wales and visit Aunt Rhonda and Uncle Huw on Wednesday. We (need) ________________ to stay at least three days in the north if we (want) ________________ to visit the main tourists spots.

ANNE: What different things can we do?

MUM: Well. It depends. You would have to decide. If you (want) ________________, we (modal + go) ________________ up Snowdon on the first day. I know how you love walking.

JAMIE: Mm, that sounds great. How high is Mount Snowdon?

MUM: Oh, 1,085 m. Some people (take) ________________ the Snowdon Mountain Railway if they (not + like) ________________ climbing up but I know you'll want to go up and down yourselves. It's much more fun anyway. On day 2 we (modal + visit) ________________ Portmeirion if you (want) ________________. It's a very special town on the north-west coast near Porthmadog. The architect wanted to build something beautiful and which fitted the countryside around it. He got many of his ideas from the Italian town, Portofino. Portmeirion became famous after a British TV company filmed the series *The Prisoner* there in the 1960s.

ANNE: Well, I'd certainly like to see it. It sounds different. And on the third day?

DAD: Well, if you (to be interested) ____________________, we (modal + go) _________ ________________ up to Caernarvon or over to Harlech Castle. Are you two interested in castles?

ANNE: Of course we are.

beach near Tenby, Wales

MUM: Well, that's decided, but then we really must go down south. There's so much there to see too. But Anne, you want to swim. If you (like) ______________________ sandy beaches, we (have to) ______________________ go to Tenby where there are lots of good beaches.

ANNE: Oh yes, mum. And on Wednesday down to Machynlleth where auntie and uncle live.

11.3 *if* und *when*

Immer wenn du *when* und *if* ins Deutsche übersetzt, musst du aufpassen: *when* = „wenn“ im Sinne von „sobald“; *if* = „wenn“ im Sinne von „falls“. Bringe sie nicht durcheinander! Allerdings stellt sich dieses Problem nur beim Gebrauch der Bedingungssätze des ersten Typs.

Beispiele: If my penfriend comes, we may go and watch a real English football match.
(= Es ist nicht 100 % sicher, dass sie /er kommt.)

When my penfriend comes, we may go and watch a real English football match.
(= Mein/e Brieffreund/in wird sicher kommen.)

If my penfriend came, we might go and watch a real English football match.
(= Ich bin mir ganz und gar nicht sicher, ob sie /er kommt.)

When my penfriend came we went and watched a real English football match.
(Mein/e Brieffreund/in ist schon hier gewesen und hat uns besucht. Hier wird *when* mit **„als“** übersetzt.)

9. **Which one?** Put either *if* or *when* in the gap in each sentence.

a) “__________ I grow up, I’ll be a fireman”, said six-year old Jack to his mother.

b) ______________ we miss the train, I’ll be angry with you.

c) I may buy myself a big box of popcorn __________ we go to the cinema tonight. Dad’s already got the tickets for us.

d) Please ring me up ____________ you get home.

e) _____________ you get home before me, please make some tea.

f) __________ I get the best mark in the geography test next week – but I don’t think I will – my parents will be pleased.

g) We'll be able to hire bikes __________ we go to Ireland on holiday next week. Mum said they're very cheap.

h) ______________ you go to Stratford-on-Avon, you must visit the house where William Shakespeare lived. Have you already made your holiday plans?

10. You. Read the following sentence halves *(if-clause)* and tick the ones which are **true (likely)** for you. Now write these sentence halves using conditional I. All the other sentences are **unlikely** for you i.e. you must write them using conditional II. Now turn the book round and find out how to complete the sentences by matching suitable endings. Write only *one sentence* for each – *either* conditional I *or* conditional II.

a) to buy some new shoes, ☐

b) to go to a football match this week, ☐

c) to go to bed late this weekend, ☐

d) to go to a party on Saturday, ☐

e) to have an English test soon, ☐

f) to find DM 50 in the road, ☐

g) to see a car accident, ☐

h) to get a summer job, ☐

i) to write a letter to my grandmother, ☐

to be very happy.
to do well.
to try and earn a lot of money.
they must be black.
nobody to mind.
to go with a friend.
to ring the police.
to have to wash my jeans.
may keep it.

a) Likely: If I buy some new shoes, they must be black.

Unlikely: If I bought some new shoes, they would have to be black.

b) ______________________________

____

c) ______________________________

____

d) ____

____

e) ____

____

f) ____

____

g) ____

____

h) ____

____

i) ____

____

12 Relativsätze

Wie du bereits weißt, besteht ein Satz aus einzelnen Wörtern, die bestimmte **Funktionen** haben und in der Grammatik mit Namen wie Verb, Adjektiv oder Nomen bedacht werden. Solche Wörter können sich auch zu Gruppen zusammenschließen und als **Teilsatz** eine besondere **Funktion im Satz** übernehmen. Die Funktion von **Relativsätzen** ist es, auf Wörter (Nomen und Pronomen) des Hauptsatzes zu verweisen und dem Leser oder Zuhörer **zusätzliche Informationen** über sie zu geben.

Rund um bestimmende und nicht bestimmende Relativsätze

Wie unterscheiden sich die Relativsätze?

Die Informationen, die in einem Relativsatz gegeben werden, können entweder **notwendig** (d.h. ohne sie weißt du nicht, wer oder was gemeint ist; der Satz macht keinen Sinn ohne sie) oder **nicht notwendig** sein (in diesem Fall könnte man den Relativsatz auch weglassen und würde den Satz trotzdem verstehen).

- Wenn der Relativsatz notwendig ist, so handelt es sich um einen **‚bestimmenden' Relativsatz.**

  Beispiel: This is the girl who discovered the fire. (notwendig)

  Der Relativsatz macht hier den Hauptsatz verständlich, indem er das Mädchen einordnet und darauf hinweist, welches Mädchen gemeint ist. Er kann nicht weggelassen werden. Bei bestimmenden Relativsätzen steht im Englischen **kein Komma!**

- Wenn der Relativsatz nicht notwendig ist und nur zusätzliche Informationen gibt, nennt man ihn einen **‚nicht bestimmenden' Relativsatz.** Er kann weggelassen werden und wird im Englischen durch **Kommas** abgetrennt.

  Beispiel: The sun, which is very bright, is shining today. (nicht notwendig)

Rund um Relativpronomen

Wie leite ich Relativsätze ein?

Ein Relativsatz wird von Wörtern wie ***who, which, that*** oder ***whose*** eingeleitet. Man nennt diese Wörter **Relativpronomen**. Sie haben die Aufgabe, das vorher genannte Nomen noch einmal zu betonen und die **beiden Satzteile miteinander zu verbinden.**

Beispiele: I have got some friends. They live in England
I have got some friends who live in England.

You were singing a song. What's the name of the song?
What's the name of the song that you were singing?

Welches Relativpronomen sollte ich verwenden?

- ***who*** bezieht sich nur auf **Personen.** *who* steht oft gleich nach Wörtern wie *man, woman, girl, boy, person, someone, anybody* usw.

  Beispiel: Alexander Bell was the man who invented the telephone.

- ***which*** bezieht sich nur auf **Dinge.**

  Beispiel: Venus is the planet which is nearest to Earth.

- ***that*** kann sich auf **Personen und Dinge** beziehen.

  Beispiele: The waitress that served me was very rude.
  The milk that I bought yesterday has already gone off.

- ***whose*** drückt **Besitz** bzw. **Zugehörigkeit** aus und bezieht sich auf **Personen, Tiere und Dinge.** *whose* übersetzt man mit „deren" oder „dessen". **Pass auf:** *whose* ist **keine alternative Schreibweise** von ***who's ... ?*** *(= who is ... ?)!*

  Beispiele: What was the name of the people whose cat got lost last Friday?
  I finished a brilliant book yesterday whose title, though, I've already forgotten!

1. Complete the following sentences by selecting the correct relative pronoun(s) *who, which, that, whose*. Sometimes only one answer is possible.

a) I know someone ___*who/that*___ has met the Queen.

b) The programme ______________________ I saw on TV last night about Australia was very interesting.

c) Can you remember the name of the restaurant ______________________ you went to on Saturday with your parents?

d) The house ______________________ was broken into last month burnt down this morning.

e) I don't like people ______________________ tell lies.

f) Do you know ______________________ book this is?

g) Did you hear about the children ______________________ found a lot of expensive jewellery last week?

h) What's the song ______________________ is Number 1 at the moment?

i) The woman ______________________ dog bit me was very sorry.

j) I went to a party last Saturday ______________________ was great fun.

- Relativpronomen können sich auf Nomen im **Plural** und im **Singular** beziehen.

Beispiele:	Do you know <u>the</u> <u>boy</u> Do you know <u>the</u> <u>people</u>	{ <u>who/</u> <u>that</u> }	lives next door? live next door?
	We've bought <u>a dog</u> We've bought <u>two</u> <u>dogs</u>	{ <u>which/</u> <u>that</u> }	barks very loudly. bark very loudly.
	We saw a man We saw <u>some</u> <u>people</u>	{ <u>whose</u> }	car had broken down.
	I know someone	{ <u>whose</u> }	sister is famous. parents are famous.

- Wenn sich ***whose*** auf Personen bezieht, ersetzt es *his/her/their*.

Beispiel: The teacher complained to the parents: <u>their</u> son never does his homework.
The teacher complained to the parents <u>whose</u> son never does his homework.

2. Explaining words. Using either <u>who</u> or <u>which</u> explain the meaning of the following words. Use these words to help you:
piece of clothing – you send – is taught – short letter – jumper – Asia - holiday – ~~wild animal~~ – Great Britain – writes – someone – part of – is made of wool – a verb – country – a person – is worn over a shirt – friend – ~~looks like~~ – scientific subject – means the same as – at schools – books – ~~a dog~~ – comes from.
Sometimes more than one answer is possible. Don't forget to add prepositions *(to/on)* and articles *(a/the)* where necessary.

a) A wolf is a wild animal which looks like a dog.

b) A pullover ______________________

c) Chemistry ______________________

d) An author ______________________

e) A postcard ______________________

f) Scotland ______________________

g) An Asian ______________________

3. Matching: Join the correct sentence halves together with a relative pronoun (*who/which/whose*).

a)	My sister works for a company			is famous for its wax figures?
b)	Have you ever met someone			won the Football World Cup in 1998?
c)	I don't know	a	which	makes films.
d)	I think it was George and Robert Stephenson			were not very expensive.
e)	What was the name of the country			car the thieves stole?
f)	What's the name of the people			attracts a lot of tourists in the summer.
g)	What's the English word for someone			can't speak English?
h)	The Lake District is a National Park in Britain			moved into that empty house last week?
i)	Can you tell me the name of the London museum			says 'Don't feed the animals', you must follow the instructions.
j)	I bought some jeans yesterday			built the first steam train.
k)	If you read a sign in a zoo			doesn't eat meat?

4. What does ... mean? Try explaining these words and pictures on your own.

a) Latin: ______________________________

b) A lifeboat: ______________________________

c)  ______________________________

d)  ______________________________

e)  ______________________________

f)  ______________________________

5. Join the following sentences together using *whose*.

a) My neighbours have got a new dog. Her name is Nellie.

My neighbours have got a new dog whose name is Nellie.

b) I saw a good film on TV last night. I've already forgotten its name.

____

c) You went to a girl's party at the weekend. What's her name?

____

d) Alan Shearer was a member of the English football team in 1998. His main job was to score goals and to be captain.

____

____

e) I borrowed a book from the library this afternoon. Its cover was already torn.

____

f) Leonardo di Caprio is a very famous actor. His face is loved by many girls.

____

6. Famous people. Encyclopaedias can give you information about famous people but it is never written in proper sentences. Read the notes about the following famous people and then write a sentence about each one. Always use a relative pronoun (*who*).

a) Beethoven, Ludwig van (1770–1827): famous German composer; *Fidelio* (opera), *Pastoral* (symphony).

Ludwig van Beethoven was a famous German composer who wrote the opera Fidelio and the symphony Pastoral.

b) Adams, John (1735–1826): President of the United States of America after George Washington.

______________________________ the man ____________________

____

c) Albert, Prince Consort (1819–61): son of the Duke of Saxe-Coburg-Gotha; married Queen Victoria 1840.

____

____

d) Baker, Sir Benjamin (1840–1897): English civil engineer, built Forth Bridge (Scotland) with Sir John Fowler and the London Metropolitan railway.

____

____

e) Burns, Robert (1759–1796): Scottish poet; among his best-known poems are *Auld Lang Syne* and *The Banks of Doon*.

____

____

7. School subjects. Look at the following table and join up the subject to the correct description.

religious knowledge	teaches us about our bodies, plants and animal life.
history	is all about numbers, fractions (¼ and ½), percentages (10%) and shapes (▲ □ ○).
geography	talks about dates, wars and people who lived a long time ago.
biology	has to do with God and what people believe in other countries.
maths	is all about other countries and the weather there and the things these countries produce.

8. Now write the complete definitions out in full using a relative pronoun (*which/that*).

a) Geography is the subject which is all about countries and the weather there and the things these countries produce.

b) Religious knowledge ____

____

c) History ____

____

d) Biology ____

____

f) Maths ____

____

Rund um *contact clauses*

Was sind *contact clauses?*

- Die *contact clauses* sind eine besondere Form der bestimmenden Relativsätze. Bei diesen Relativsätzen kann man, anders als im Deutschen, das **Relativpronomen weglassen.** Du kannst das Relativpronomen nur dann weglassen, wenn es **Objekt des Relativsatzes** (und nicht Subjekt) ist. Lasse also das Relativpronomen **nie wegfallen,** wenn es **Subjekt** des Relativsatzes ist.

  Beispiele: My little sister broke the CD (that) I bought last week.
  (*that* ist Objekt von *bought.)*
  The boy (who) I met at the disco on Saturday is called David.
  (*who* ist Objekt von *met.)*

- Die nachfolgende Tabelle zeigt dir nun, wie man diese besondere Art der Relativsätze erkennt und wie man Objekt- und Subjektpronomen auseinanderhält.

	Relativsatz			
Hauptsatz	**Objekt** (Frage: wen oder was?)	**Subjekt** (Frage: wer oder was?)		Hauptsatz
The English book	*(which/ that)*	*I*	*am reading*	is very difficult.
A girl	*(who/ that)*	*I*	*know*	doesn't like it either.
A book		*which/ that*	*is easier to read*	is *The Pig Man.*
The girl		*who/ that*	*gave me this book*	is called Trish.

✷ **9. Two into one.** Join these sentences together to form one sentence *without* using a relative pronoun. Notice that you will usually need to change the indefinite article (*a/an*) into the definite article (*the*) in the new sentence.

a) You lost a door key yesterday. Have you found it?
Have you found the door key you lost yesterday?

b) I bought some shoes last month. They've already got a hole in them.

____

c) We tried to go to a film yesterday. It was sold out.

____

d) There's a new pupil in our class. I don't like her.

____

e) We met an English family last year. The family have invited us to visit them.

____

f) Peter bought a new CD on Monday. I would like to borrow it.

____

g) Pat is wearing new glasses. They look nice.

____

h) My uncle tells me stories. They are always funny.

____

10. The Channel Islands: contact clause or not? Read the following text and decide whether to include a relative pronoun or not. If a relative pronoun is necessary, choose the correct one and write it in the gap.

The Channel Islands are small islands ________________ lie off the north–west coast of France. The political situation is one ___________ is interesting because the islands do not belong to Great Britain i. e. England, Scotland and Wales but to the British Isles (Great Britain, Northern Ireland and 5,000 other smaller islands). The language of the people _____________ live in the islands is English and not French, something _____________ a lot of tourists believe.
The largest island is Jersey ______________ zoo is famous because of all the exotic and rare animals. The first owner of the zoo was a well-known author ________________ name was Gerald Durrell. Jersey is 117 km^2. The second

largest island (65 km^2) is Guernsey ______________ is historically famous because the French author Victor Hugo lived there after he had to leave France. There are three other main islands ______________ all belong to Guernsey: Alderney (8 km^2), Sark (5 km^2) has two parts (Big Sark and Little Sark); Herm (1.3 km^2). The other four smaller ones are Jethou, Lihou, Brecqhou and Burnou.
The islands first belonged to England in 1066 when William The Conqueror (______________was the Duke of Normandy) beat the English at the Battle of Hastings and became King of England. When Queen Elizabeth II visits the islands, she has another title: the Duchess of Normandy.
1973 is another date ______________ is historically important: the islands voted not to join the European Union (then called the European Economic Community [EEC]). The main industry ______________ the islands have is tourism: thousands of tourists visit every year because of the warm weather, golden beaches and blue water. The islands are famous for the rich milk ___________ their cows make.

beach on Jersey Island

Jersey and Guernsey have their own currency and stamps. The pictures on the coins, notes and stamps are not the same as the ones ______________ Britain has. The islands have their own governments ________________ means they have no MP in London. There is no Prime Minister in Guernsey or Jersey. The 'leaders' of the islands have a title ______________ comes from French – 'Bailiff'. Only someone ______________ is from the islands can do the job.

It's easy to visit the Channel Islands because the three largest ones each have an airport. Another method ___________ you can use to get there is boat. Now you just have to decide on the name of the island ___________ you and your family would like to visit!

Rund um Relativsätze mit Präpositionen

Wohin stellst du die Präposition im Satz?

- In Relativsätzen verwendet man sehr häufig Präpositionen, wie z. B. *for, in, on, at, with.* Auch *contact clauses* können Präpositionen enthalten.

  Beispiele: Do you know the name of the new pupil (who/that) Kathryn is talking to?
  The village in which I live is a little bit boring.
  The date (which/that) I was born on is a public holiday – the first of January.

- In Sätzen, in denen man das Relativpronomen **weglassen kann** *(contact clauses),* steht die Präposition ganz am **Ende** des Relativsatzes.

  Beispiele: The party (which/that) I went to last night was great fun.
  The woman whose flat we live in is French.
  The policeman (who/that) I spoke to was very helpful.

- In **förmlichem Englisch** (z. B. beim Schreiben) setzt man das Relativpronomen ein, selbst wenn es nicht unbedingt nötig ist. In diesem Fall steht die Präposition unmittelbar **vor** dem Relativpronomen.

  Beispiel: The party to which I went last night was great fun.

- Stellt man aber in förmlichem Englisch eine Präposition vor das Relativpronomen *who,* dann verändert sich *who* zu *whom.* Dies ist die besondere **Objektform** von *who* und wird nur in geschriebenem Englisch benutzt.

  Beispiel: The woman to whom I spoke was very helpful.

- *that* steht **nie nach einer Präposition:** Du kannst nur die gewöhnliche Konstruktion benutzen.

  Beispiel: The woman that I spoke to was very helpful.

11. One plus one equals one. Join the following sentences using a *relative clause construction.* Use the *informal style* (preposition after the relative pronoun).

a) We live in a flat. It's very noisy.
The flat which/that we live in is very noisy.

b) My parents went on holiday last month. It was terrible.
____

c) David's sister lives in a small village. It's quite near Manchester.
____

d) I spent an hour in hospital yesterday with my friend. She broke her leg in a bicycle accident.
____

e) Julie ran into a car. The car was not damaged badly.
____

f) I painted my bedroom with two friends. They're called Sam and Fiona.
____

g) We went to an interesting castle in northern England. It is called Castle Howard.
____

h) I slept in my new bed last night. It is very comfortable.
____

12. The Royal Family. How much do you know about them? Complete these sentences using the *formal style.* Add the correct preposition and relative pronoun.

a) Do you know the name of the palace in which the Queen lives?

b) What's the name of the school ____________ Prince William and Harry go?

c) ____________ country does the Royal Family stay when they are on their summer holidays?

d) Do you know the date ____________ Princess Diana was killed?

e) Do you know _________________ year the Queen Mother was born?

f) Can you tell me _________________ country Prince Philip originally comes?

g) _________________ animals does the Queen spend a lot of time?

h) Have you any idea ___________________ which sport Prince Charles is very good?

i) Can you tell me ___________________ years the Queen's children were born?

j) _________________ village and _________________ county was Princess Diana buried?

k) _________________ famous horserace do all the royal women wear big, expensive hats?

13. Answering questions. Using the clues in the box answer the questions in 12. Make your answers short and use personal pronouns to replace the subject and/or object.

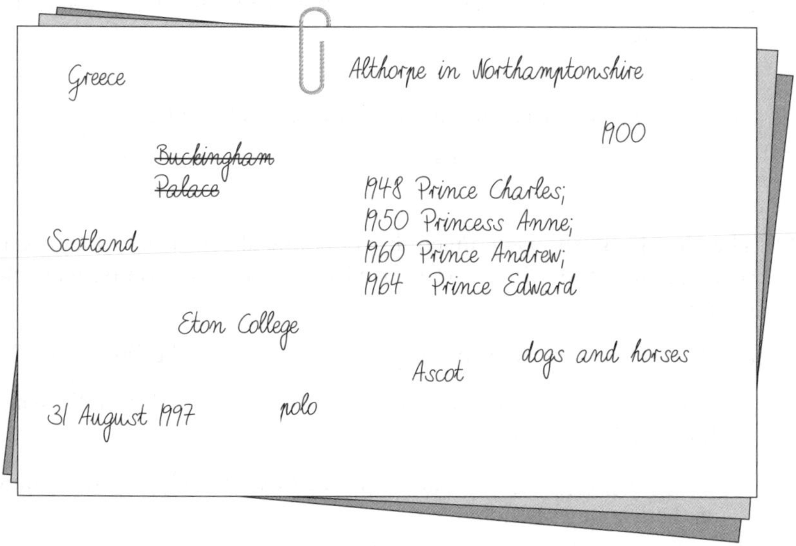

a) She lives in Buckingham Palace.

b) ______________________________

c) ______________________________

d) ______________________________

e) ______________________________

f) ______________________________

g) ______________________________

h) ______________________________

i) ______________________________

j) ______________________________

k) ______________________________

14. Edinburgh. Complete this text using relative clauses and prepositions as necessary. If you think it is unnecessary to include the relative pronoun, put brackets ( ) around it.

This is the name of the city ______________ is the capital of Scotland. The river ___________ it is built on is the Forth. Edinburgh is on the eastern side of Scotland. James IV was the King ______________ began the royal palace at Holyroodhouse in 1500. There are several famous people ____________ came from Edinburgh. The one __________ name is the best known is Sir Walter Scott. Two well- known books ___________ he wrote are

Rob Roy and *Ivanhoe*. The city is one of Europe's main cultural centres. The Edinburgh Festival, _________________ thousands of people come _________________ every year, has become one of the world's most important festivals of music and drama. The city has got a university ____________ is very old and some other important buildings, for example national art galleries and the Scott Monument. Some of the industries ______________ Edinburgh is well-known ______________ are printing, publishing and electronics equipment. The city has a population _________ is approximately 450,000.

13 Schwierige Wörter, die wir in diesem Buch benutzen

abbey	– Abtei
acre	– Flächeneinheit
(to) add (a building)	– *hier:* anbauen (z. B. Gebäude)
Anglo-Norman	– anglo-normannisch
(to) answer the phone	– das Telefon abheben, ans Telefon gehen
approximately	– circa, etwa, ungefähr
architect	– Architekt
(to) arrest	– jmdn. festnehmen
art gallery	– Kunstgalerie
artist	– Künstler
audience	– Publikum
baggage	– Gepäck
bailiff	– Gerichtsvollzieher, Hilfsbeamter
barbecue party	– Grillparty
barn	– Scheune
basket	– Korb
battle	– 1) Kampf; 2) Schlacht
(to) beat	– 1) gewinnen (gegen); 2) schlagen
bell	– Glocke
(to) belong to	– gehören zu
bench	– Bank (zum Sitzen)
(to) bet	– wetten
(to) bleed	– bluten
(to) boil	– kochen
borough	– Stadtbezirk
(inner) borough	– Stadtbezirk um die 'City' von London herum
(outer) borough	– Stadtbezirk am Rand von London
brackets	– Klammer
(to) brake	– bremsen

(to) break away from sth	–	aus etwas ausbrechen
(to) break down	–	zusammenbrechen
briefly	–	kurz
brilliant, brilliantly	–	brillant
British Top Thirty charts	–	Top 30 Hitparade
(to) brush	–	bürsten
building	–	Gebäude
(to) bury	–	begraben
business reasons	–	geschäftliche Gründe
button	–	Knopf
camp fire	–	Lagerfeuer
camp	–	Heerlager
career	–	Karriere
castle	–	1) Schloss; 2) Burg
cellar	–	Keller
century	–	Jahrhundert
change	–	*hier:* Änderung
Channel Tunnel, the	–	Der Kanaltunnel
chapel	–	Kapelle
chess	–	Schach
choir	–	Chor
circle	–	Kreis
Cistercian monk	–	Zisterzienser Mönch
civil engineer	–	Bauingenieur
(to) clear the table	–	den Tisch abdecken
cockerel	–	Hahn
coin	–	Münze
college	–	Hochschule
comb	–	Kamm
(to) come round (to s.o.'s house)	–	vorbeikommen
(to) complain	–	sich beschweren
(to) complete	–	vervollständigen
composer	–	Komponist
(to) concern	–	mit etwas zu tun haben, etwas betreffen
condition	–	*hier:* Bedingung
conditions	–	Verhältnisse
Conservative Party	–	Konservative Partei

(to) continue	– fortfahren
cookery lesson	– Kochkurs
cottage	– kleines Haus
county	– Grafschaft
cover	– Umschlag
crossroads	– Kreuzung
(to) crown	– jmdn. krönen
cultural centre	– Kulturzentrum
(to) **d**amage,	– beschädigen
deadline	– Abgabetermin
death	– Tod
(to) decorate	– *hier:* schmücken
decoration	– Schmuck, Dekoration
deer	– Reh
dinosaur	– Dinosaurier
(to) disappear	– verschwinden
(to) discover	– entdecken
donkey	– Esel
dozen	– 12, ein Dutzend
drive	– Einfahrt
drums	– Schlagzeug
Duchess	– Herzogin
Duke	– Herzog
(to) **e**arn,	– verdienen
electricity	– Elektrizität, Strom, Stromquelle
electronics equipment	– elektronische Ausstattung
(to) empty	– entleeren
encyclopaedia	– Enzyklopädie
engineer	– Ingenieur
etc.	– usw.
European Economic Community (EEC)	– die Europäische Wirtschaftsgemeinschaft
European Union	– die Europäische Gemeinschaft
event	– Ereignis
exchange	– *hier:* Austauschschüler
excuse	– Ausrede

exile (to be in ...)	– im Exil leben
exotic	– exotisch
expansion	– Ausdehnung
(to) expect	– erwarten
famous (to be ... for)	– berühmt sein
fancy dress party	– Party mit Verkleidungszwang
fashionable	– modisch
female	– weiblich
(to) fit	– passen
flat	– flach
flood	– die Flut
(to) flood	– überfluten
flour	– Mehl
foot soldier	– Fusssoldat
football boots	– Fußballschuhe
football ground	– Fußballplatz
foreigner	– Ausländer
fraction	– Bruchteil
freezer	– Gefriertruhe
freezing cold	– eiskalt
fruit (tinned)	– Früchte (in der Dose)
furniture	– Möbel
(to) **g**amble	– spielen (Glücksspiel)
gap	– Lücke
garage	– 1) Garage; 2) Werkstatt; 3) Tankstelle
(to) get home	– zu Hause ankommen
(to) get ready	– vorbereiten
(to) go off (milk, meat, etc.)	– verderben, schlecht werden (Milch, Fleisch usw.)
(to) go with	– zusammenpassen
government	– Regierung
(to) guess	– raten
guide book	– Reiseführer
guide	– Reiseführer

hairstyle	– Haarschnitt, Frisur
harbour	– Hafen
hardly	– kaum
(to) have to do with	– mit etwas zu tun haben
hay	– Heu
head	– 1) Kopf; 2) Chef einer Partei; 3) Leiter einer Abteilung
heading	– Überschrift, Titel
headline	– Schlagzeile
helpless	– hilflos
hero	– ausleihen
historical	– historisch
hit	– Hit
(to) hit	– 1) schlagen; 2) treffen
horserace	– Pferderennen
i.e.	– d. h.
ID card	– Ausweispapiere
(to) imagine	– sich etwas vorstellen
(to) include	– 1) einschließen; 2) beinhalten
incomprehensible	– unverständlich
independent	– unabhängig
(the) Industrial Revolution	– die Industrielle Revolution
(to) influence	– beeinflussen
inner	– inner(halb)
international	– international
(to) introduce	– einführen
(to) invent	– erfinden
IQ	– Intelligenzquotient
item	– ein Gegenstand
jewellery	– Schmuck
job	– 1) Arbeit; 2) Aufgabe
(to) join	– sich anschließen
journey	– Reise
jumper	– Pullover
(to) **k**nit	– stricken
knowledge	– Wissen

Labour Party	– Arbeiterpartei
lad	– Bursche
(to) lay the table	– den Tisch decken
leader	– Führer
(to) lie off	– vor der Küste liegen
life line	– hier: Lebenslauf in Tabellenform
local person	– Ortsansässiger
(to) lock oneself out (of)	– sich ausschließen (aus dem Haus/der Wohnung)
luggage	– Gepäck
(to) **m**ake s.o. do sth	– jmdn. dazu bringen, etw. zu tun
male	– männlich
maritime	– alles, was mit dem Meer zu tun hat
(to) mark	– 1) make a sign; 2) korrigieren, benoten
(to be) married	– verheiratet sein
(to get) married	– heiraten
match	– Spiel
(to) match	– miteinander abstimmen
medieval	– mittelalterlich
(to) melt	– schmelzen
member	– 1) Mitglied; 2) Teilnehmer
(to) mend	– reparieren
menu	– Karte (im Restaurant)
message	– Nachricht
method	– 1) Möglichkeit; 2) Methode
(to) milk	– melken
(to) mix	– mischen
moat	– Burggraben
monastery	– Kloster
monk	– Mönch
monument	– Denkmal
(to) move in(to)	– einziehen
MP (Member of Parliament)	– Mitglied des Parlaments
murderer	– Mörder
musical instrument	– Musikinstrument

night-club	–	Nachtclub
note	–	1) Geldschein; 2) Notiz
nun	–	Nonne
official	–	offiziell
opera	–	Oper
original, originally	–	ursprünglich
outer	–	äußerer, -e, -es
painting	–	Bild
part	–	1) Teil; 2) Rolle (Theaterstück, usw.)
particular	–	besonders
part-time job	–	Halbtagsjob
passenger	–	Passagier
path	–	Pfad
pepper	–	Pfeffer
percentage	–	Prozentsatz
perfume	–	Perfüm
plain buiscuit	–	einfacher Keks
(to) plan	–	1) planen; 2) vorhaben
planner	–	Planer
plant	–	Pflanze
(to) plant	–	pflanzen
platform	–	Gleis
poet	–	Dichter
political	–	politisch
porridge	–	Haferbrei ähnliches Frühstück
port	–	Hafen
pot	–	1) Tee- oder Kaffeekanne; 2) Topf
pottery	–	Töpferei
power (to be under s.o.'s ...)	–	in jmds Macht sein
(to) prefer	–	bevorziehen
(to) prepare	–	vorbereiten
priest	–	Priester
Prime Minister	–	Premierminister
printing	–	Druck
(to) produce	–	produzieren
programme (TV)	–	Sendung
proper, properly	–	richtig

property	– Besitz
public holiday	– Feiertag
publishing	– Veröffentlichung
purple	– lila
purpose	– Grund
race	– Rennen
rare	– selten
recipe	– Rezept
record	– 1) Schallplatte; 2) Rekord
religious	– religiös
(to) remove	– entfernen
(to) replace	– ersetzen
report	– Bericht
(to) ring out	– ausläuten
(to) rise	– *hier:* aufgehen
road to success	– der Weg zum Erfolg
Roman	– Römer
(to) run through	– fließen
scandalous	– skandalös
scientific	– wissenschaftlich
scientist	– Wissenschaftler
scissors	– Schere
(to) score a goal	– ein Tor schießen
section	– 1) Sektion; 2) Abteilung
(to) select	– auswählen
(to) sentence s.o. to death	– jdn. zum Tode verurteilen
separate	– getrennt
series	– *hier:* eine TV Serie
(to) set up sth	– etw. aufbauen
(to) sew	– nähen
shape	– Form
sheepdog	– Hirtenhund
shell	– Muschel
(to) shoot to	– hochschnellen
(to) siege	– belagern
(to) sink	– sinken
slice	– Scheibe (Wurst, Brot usw.)
(to) slip	– ausrutschen

snail – Schnecke mit Haus
sold out (to sell out) – ausverkauft sein
spider – Spinne
sports coach – Trainer
steam train – Dampflok
step (front step) – Eingangstreppe
strawberry – Erdbeere
successful – erfolgreich
suitable – passend
supper – Abendessen
(to) surprise – überraschen
sword – Schwert
symphony – Sinfonie

(to) **t**ake care – aufpassen
tie – Krawatte
toothpaste – Zahnpasta
torn (to tear) – zerrissen (zerreißen)
tortoise – Schildkröte
tourism – Tourismus
tower – Turm
tradition – Tradition
trial – Gerichtsverhandlung
triple jumper – Dreispringer
tube (by ...) – 1) (mit der) U- oder S-Bahn; 2) Tube
(to) type – tippen

(to) **u**nderline – unterstreichen
unemployed – arbeitslos
university – Universität
up till now – bis jetzt

valuable – wertvoll
verb scale – Verbskala
(to) vote – wählen (bei einer politischen Wahl)

waitress – Kellnerin
(to) water – gießen
waterfront – die Front

wax figure	–	Wachsfigur
William the Conqueror	–	William der Eroberer
wish	–	Wunsch
witch	–	Hexe
World Cup	–	Weltmeisterschaft
worm	–	Wurm
yard	–	1) 0.91 m; 2) Hof

Lösungen

Plural

1. a) The cats have caught some mice.
b) Our wives have got sharp knives in their kitchens.
c) Some children were playing with some geese.
d) The wolves are eating some brown and white calves.
e) Are their lives interesting?
f) One half? No, two halves, please.
g) Our teeth hurt.
h) The thieves stole some loaves of bread.
i) Those men are very rich.
j) We hurt ourselves this morning.
k) What trees are those leaves from?
l) Have some shelves fallen down?

2. a) The police haven't (have not) given us any information.
b) The news she gave me was interesting.
c) I caught/was able to catch three fish yesterday./Yesterday I caught/was able to catch three fish.
d) Susannah's new glasses are very nice.
e) Could you give me some advice about/advise me/tell me where I can buy cheap furniture?
f) There are always lots of flies in summer./In summer there are always a lot of flies.
g) My jeans were expensive.
h) These scissors aren't particularly sharp.
i) I'd like two kilos of tomatoes, please./Can I/Could I/May I have two kilos of tomatoes, please?
j) The farmer has bought two donkeys. They are very loud!
k) My clothes are a bit/a little dirty.
l) The rubbish smells awful/terrible/dreadful.
m) The sheep in the mountains have got a hard life.
n) Your holiday photos/The photos of your holiday are good.

Unbestimmte Pronomen und Begleiter: *some* and *any*

1. a) some, some, some
b) any, any, some
c) some
d) any, some
e) some/any

2. anything, something, anyone/anybody, someone/somebody, anyone/anybody, someone/somebody, Anywhere, some, Anybody/Anyone, some, any

Das Stützwort one

1. a) famous one
b) other ones
c) easy one
d) successful, ones
e) useful one
f) fashionable one
g) important ones
h) unusual ones
i) classical, popular ones
j) scandalous ones
k) sad ones, happy ones, love ones

2. a) French one, the Swiss one, the Swiss one
b) fruit ones, the natural ones, the fruit ones
c) the red ones, the green ones, the red ones
d) the Indian one, the Chinese one, the Chinese one
e) the chocolate ones, the plain ones, the chocolate ones
f) the brown ones, the white ones, the brown ones
g) the cheap one, the expensive one, the expensive one

3. the, the, the, A, —, the, —

4. a) I don't like the way the cat looks/is looking at the moment. The poor thing/animal must go to the vet's.
b) The only thing in this game which is complicated is the beginning/start.
or
The only complicated thing about this game is the beginning/start.
c) The police have got a difficult case to solve: they've found an unknown dead person/man.
d) Tina has got a very close relationship with her grandparents: the small/little girl spends every weekend there.
e) Nobody knew who the poor man was.
f) The new girl in our class comes from Berlin.
g) The interesting thing is that nobody saw who threw the stone.

5. a) the one
b) the, —
c) The ones
d) —
e) —, —, —, the one
f) one
g) —, ones, The ones

6. a) Which cat, The black one
b) Which —/one, The mountain bike
c) Which CD player, The (more) expensive one, the cheap(er) one, The cheap(er) one
d) Which t-shirt/one, This (one), prefer that (one)
e) Which postcard/one, send the River Thames one

Wie Wörter gebildet werden

1. a) rain

b) snow

c) cloud

d) fog

e) sun

2. "Good evening, this is Lana Roberts with the weather report until tomorrow evening. There's heavy fog in the Norfolk area and there will be no change until midday tomorrow. Here in London it's cool and cloudy. No rain is expected until tomorrow night. Up in rainy Scotland it doesn't seem the weather is ever going to change. I'm afraid it's not a good day for going outside. Out on the south-west coast it's warm and sunny. The sun just won't stop shining. In the north-east of England the windy conditions are causing big problems at sea. The wind is expected to become less strong by tomorrow morning. The clouds over the Midlands will disappear by midday. Tomorrow afternoon will be warm with perhaps a little rain in the evening. Now briefly over to Europe. In southern Germany the weather is perfect for skiing: lots of snow but also sunny. We expect these snowy conditions to continue all this week .... That's all for today. Good night."

3.

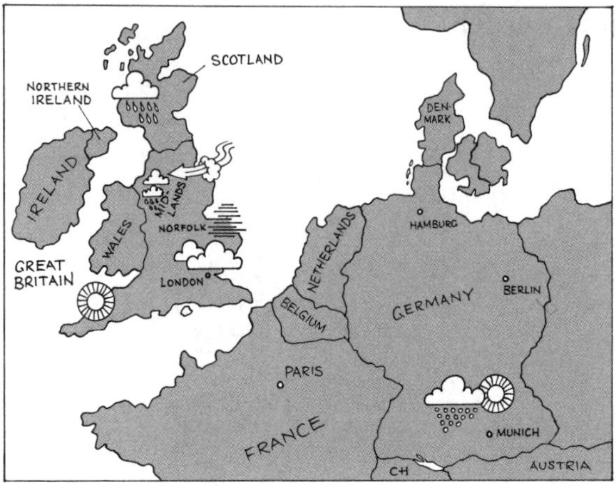

4/5

noun	translation	adjective	translation
storm	Sturm	stormy	stürmisch
smell	Gestank/Geruch	smelly	stinkend
noise	Lärm	noisy	laut
fun	Spaß	funny	lustig/komisch/ seltsam
hunger	Hunger	hungry	hungrig
juice	Saft	juicy	saftig
thirst	Durst	thirsty	durstig
sun	Sonne	sunny	sonnig
rock	Felsen	rocky	felsig
salt	Salz	salty	salzig
sandy	Sand	sandy	sandig

Aufgepasst: *Smell* kann eine **neutrale** Bedeutung („Geruch") oder eine **negative** („Gestank") haben. Das Adjektiv *smelly* hat immer negative Bedeutung. Ähnlich: *fun* bedeutet nur ‚Spaß' während *funny* entweder mit „lustig/komisch" oder mit „seltsam/komisch" übersetzt werden kann.

6. a) noisy neighbours
b) icy road/street
c) smelly socks
d) stormy sea

7.

verb	adjective	prefix + adjective
to agree	agreeable	unagreeable/disagreeable
to break	breakable	unbreakable
to change	changeable	unchangeable
to forget	forgettable	unforgettable
to imagine	imaginable	unimaginable
to like	likeable	unlikeable
to love	lovable	unlovable
to reason	reasonable	unreasonable
to sink	sinkable	unsinkable
to think	thinkable	unthinkable

8. a) washable
b) readable
c) likeable
d) unimaginable
e) unbeatable
f) lovable
g) unthinkable
h) breakable
i) unforgettable
j) enjoyable

The hidden word is: believable

9. a) rider
b) listener
c) traveller
d) singer
e) interviewer
f) dreamer
g) gambler
h) climber
i) swimmer
j) builder

10. a watchmaker is someone who makes watches
a newsreader is someone who reads (the) news
a storyteller is someone who tells stories
a weight lifter is someone who lifts weights

11. a) reporter
b) rider
c) painter
d) climber
e) skier

12. a) A reporter needs a tape recorder/a notebook/a pencil to report.
b) A rider needs a saddle/a horse/riding boots to ride.
c) A painter needs paint/a bucket/a ladder/a paintbrush to paint.
d) A climber needs a compass/a rope/climbing (walking) boots to climb.
e) A skier needs a ski suit/skis/ski boots to ski.

13.

b	e	z	f	a	c	u	n	r	e	a	d	a	b	l	e
r	i	p	l	o	s	m	e	l	l	y	i	e	e	i	s
e	i	w	u	s	i	n	g	e	r	m	r	o	o	s	u
a	n	p	a	i	n	t	g	a	f	l	t	a	s	t	n
k	t	h	i	n	k	s	r	j	o	p	r	i	d	e	n
a	e	d	f	s	a	h	i	u	r	t	h	r	o	n	y
b	r	e	a	d	l	f	n	i	g	w	i	n	n	e	r
l	v	i	s	i	t	o	r	c	e	i	m	o	n	r	g
e	i	n	h	a	t	g	s	y	t	n	o	i	t	i	o
f	e	t	s	o	s	i	l	o	l	d	p	s	a	l	t
s	w	i	m	m	e	r	b	i	c	y	d	e	o	l	t
c	e	u	n	d	e	r	s	t	a	n	d	a	b	l	e
y	r	a	i	n	y	a	b	l	m	a	t	z	e	r	l

Adjektive

1.

small	smaller	(the) smallest
hot	hotter	(the) hottest
far	further	(the) furthest
busy	busier	(the) busiest
white	whiter	(the) whitest
sweet	sweeter	(the) sweetest
clever	cleverer	(the) cleverest
friendly	friendlier	(the) friendliest
old	older	(the) oldest
bad	worse	(the) worst

2. a) colder
b) easier
c) more expensive
d) the closest
e) older
f) the most exciting/interesting
g) better
h) less
i) the most intelligent/the cleverest
j) uglier
k) lightest

3. a) bigger
b) better
c) the fastest
d) more careful
e) slower

4. a) taller than, isn't as tall as
b) friendlier than, isn't as friendly as
c) further than, as far as
d) as expensive as, isn't as expensive as, cheaper than

e) dirtier than, isn't as dirty as

f) later than, as early as

5. nicer, more expensive, more fashionable, taller, the smallest

6. more difficult, the highest, more fun/more exciting, more exciting/more fun, nicer/friendlier/more friendly, more friendly/friendlier/nicer, the best/the nicest

7. a) faster
b) better
c) laziest
d) worse
e) longer
f) colder
g) smallest
h) heavier
i) least
j) prettiest

Hidden word: friendlier

8. a) A horse is larger than a pony.

b) An adult is older than a teenager.

c) The Nile is longer than the Rhein.

d) A sofa is more comfortable than a bench.

e) A road is wider than a path.

f) £10 is more valuable than DM 10.

g) A motorbike is more dangerous than a bicycle.

h) A 5p coin is smaller than a £1 coin.

i) Fresh fruit is healthier/more healthy than tinned fruit.

9. a) 0° Celsius isn't as cold as 0° Fahrenheit.

b) A metre is longer than a yard.

c) 1 lb isn't as heavy as 1 kg.

d) DM 1 is less valuable than £1.

e) 10 miles is as far as 16 km.

10. a) Oliver is the heaviest of the three.

b) Emma is older than Oliver./Oliver isn't as old as Emma.

c) Emma is the most intelligent of the three./Oliver is the least intelligent of the three.
d) William is taller than Nathalie./Nathalie isn't as tall as William.
e) Oliver is heavier than Emma./Emma isn't as heavy as Oliver.
f) Oliver is tallest of the three.
g) William is the youngest of the three.
h) William is more intelligent than Oliver./Oliver is less intelligent than William.
i) Nathalie is the lightest of the three.
j) Emma is more intelligent than Nathalie./Nathalie is less intelligent than Emma./Nathalie isn't as intelligent as Emma.

11. a) looks
b) smells
c) tastes
d) sounds
e) feel, feel

12. a) good
b) carefully
c) awful/horrible
d) well
e) stupid
f) nice
g) slowly
h) loud
i) carefully
j) horrible/awful
k) funny

13. a) sounds awful/terrible/horrible
b) don't feel (very) well
c) tastes/smells bad/horrible/terrible/awful
d) sounds awful/horrible/terrible
e) tastes delicious/nice/good
f) smells nice/good/beautiful
g) doesn't feel (very) well
h) look good/nice
i) feel soft/nice/good or smell nice/good
j) don't look (very) well

Adverbien

1.

German	adjective	adverb
durstig	thirsty	thirstily
schnell	quick/fast	quickly/fast
möglich	possible	possibly
spät	late	late
freundlich	friendly	in a friendly way
ruhig	quiet	quietly
hungrig	hungry	hungrily
böse/verärgert	angry	angrily
hart/schwer	hard	hard
gut	good	well
nervös	nervous	nervously

2. a) quickly, fast
b) good
c) nervous, well
d) possible, hard, angry
e) nervously
f) possibly, hard

3.

a)	slow	slowly	more slowly	most slowly
	fast	fast	faster	fastest
b)	stupid	stupidly	more stupidly	most stupidly
	clever	cleverly	more cleverly	most cleverly
c)	quiet	quietly	more quietly	most quietly
	loud	loudly	more loudly	most loudly
d)	late	late	later	latest
	early	early	earlier	earliest
e)	good	well	better	best
	bad	badly	worse	worst
f)	easy	easily	more easily	most easily
	hard	hard	harder	hardest

g)	happy	happily	more happily	most happily
	sad	sadly	sadder	saddest
h)	careful	carefully	more carefully	most carefully
	dangerous	dangerously	more dangerously	most dangerously

4. a) carefully, more carefully
b) early, earlier
c) slowly, the most slowly
d) much, the most
e) well, much better
f) quietly, more quietly

5. a) good, further than
b) impolitely, more politely, more sensible
c) powerfully, more powerfully, the best
d) the fastest, earlier

6. a) She can still play tennis better than Martina Hingis.
Martina Hingis can't play tennis as well as her.
b) drives as dangerously as Michael Schumacher.
c) jump further than anyone else.
can jump further than him.
d) (football) more successfully than Newcastle United at the moment.
(football) as successfully as Arsenal at the moment.
e) can run faster/more quickly than most other 400 m runners
Most other 400 m runners can't run faster than her/as quickly/fast as her.
Most other 400 m runners run less quickly than her.
f) The Australian *Wallabies* team doesn't play as strongly as the New Zealand *All Blacks* rugby team.
The Australian *Wallabies* team plays less strongly than the New Zealand *All Blacks* rugby team.

7. the most famous, bravely, as easily as, strong, more successfully than, most important, fiercely, bigger than, bravest, the best, better than, further than, cleverly, difficult, less successfully, terrible, big, better, successfully, more modern than, larger

Zeitformen des Verbs

1.

present progressive				
zeitlich begrenzte Handlung	zeitlich begrenzter Zeitraum	zeitlich begrenzte Gewohnheit	bedauernswerte Angewohnheit	Ausnahme
e)	b)	a)	k)	j)
	d)			o)

simple present				
unveränderliche Sachverhalte	Angewohnheit, regelmäßige Aktivität	allgemein wahre Begebenheit	wissenschaftliche Erkenntnis	Allgemeinplatz
i)	c)	f)	f)	g)
	h)	l)	m)	n)
	p)			

2. a) is trying
b) I'm learning, is teaching
c) lives, do your grandparents live
d) isn't working
e) usually grows, isn't growing
f) is learning, is, has got
g) go
h) is coming
i) goes
j) Does it ever snow
k) is, is growing
l) plays
m) gets

3. a) My name is Lesley Croucher.
b) I live in Nördlingen. I live in a town/small village near Frankfurt. I live near Chemnitz.
c) I've got 1 sister and 2 brothers./I've got a twin brother./I haven't got any brothers or sisters: I'm an only child.
d) I prefer French and sport.
e) I don't like biology.

f) Yes, I do./No, I don't .
I practise every day/once a week/three times a week.

g) I listen to techno, *B*witched* and *die Ärzte*.

h) Yes, I am./No, I'm not.
I go twice a week.

i) I get up at 6 o'clock and I go to bed at 9 o'clock.

4. I'm having, have got, are, feed, is staying, I'm doing, prefer, are, jumps, are getting, have got, Do you remember, lives, is always making, wake up, know, hate

5. Fred is staying with his grandmother in her flat because his mother is in hospital. Normally he lives in a house with his mum, sister and their cat, Mog. Fred is in the 3rd year at his school. He doesn't like school much but he loves the school band. He plays the drums: he can play very well. But his grandmother's neighbours think he plays too loudly. At the moment he's practising for the school Christmas concert. He practises three times a week. The neighbours often say: "That boy! He's always playing those drums. Why doesn't he do his homework, that's much quieter?"

6.

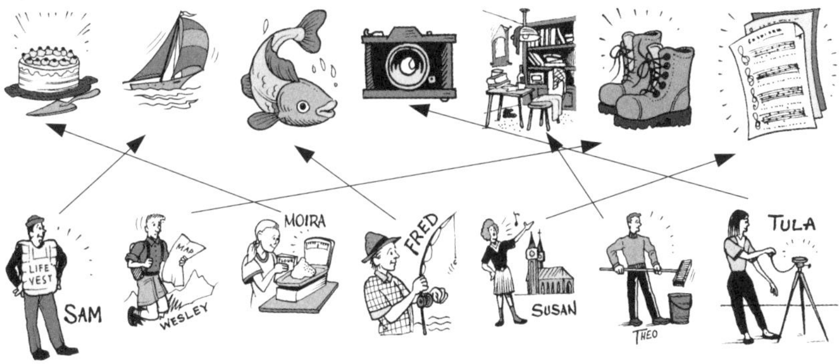

a) Moira is making a cake on Monday.

b) Tula is taking photos on Tuesday.

c) Wesley is walking in Wales on Wednesday.

d) Theo is tidying up his room on Thursday.

e) Fred is fishing on Friday.

f) Sam is sailing on Saturday.

g) Susan is singing in church on Sunday.

7. a) When are you leaving? ≈ I'm leaving on Monday.

b) Are you going alone? ≈ No, (I'm not,) I'm going with Andy.

c) Where are you meeting him? ≈ I'm meeting him/We're meeting at his house at 8 a.m./8 o's clock.

d) Where are you going on the first day? ≈ We're going to Canterbury.

e) How long are you staying in Canterbury? ≈ We're (only) staying one night.

f) What's the name of the last town you're cycling to? ≈ The last town we're cycling to is Oxford.

g) When are you coming home? ≈ We are coming home/arriving back on Sunday.

8.

Simple Past				
Bestimmte Zeit in der Vergangenheit	Ereignis, das ständig in der Vergangenheit stattfindet	Wiederholtes Ereignis (Angewohnheit) in der Vergangenheit	Geschichte in der Vergangenheit	Zeitindikator *when*
f)	e)	d)	a)	h)

Present Perfect		
Nicht abgeschlossener Vorgang ohne Änderungen	Nicht abgeschlossener Vorgang in bestimmter Zeit	Vorgang mit noch sichtbaren Folgen
b)	g)	c)

9. a) He has just gone to the dentist.

b) We've already made the beds for you, mum.

c) I still haven't done it.

d) Haven't you seen *Titanic* yet?

e) Has Mr Chapman already marked our homework?

f) Have you just had a bath?

g) They haven't yet decided what to do./They haven't decided what to do yet.

h) Hasn't she already read it?

10. a) Er ist gerade zum Zahnarzt gegangen.

b) Wir haben schon die Betten für dich gemacht, Mama.

c) Ich habe es immer noch nicht gemacht.

d) Hast du *Titanic* noch nicht gesehen?

e) Hat Mr Chapman unsere Hausaufgaben schon korrigiert?

f) Hast du gerade gebadet?

g) Sie haben sich noch nicht entschieden, was sie machen werden/wollen.

h) Hat sie es nicht schon gelesen?

11. a) died, was, wrote, have read

b) thought, were, took, agreed, started, still haven't accepted

c) Have you ever heard, have, have read, read, did you know, was, didn't, left, arrived, was, visited, was, visited, was, was, wrote, died, has ever forgotten

12. a) has been painting

b) has never read

c) has been crying

d) have happened, have been driving

e) Have you been waiting

f) still hasn't decided

g) I've been working

h) Hasn't Stuart told, yet

i) has just finished, have already read

j) has been making, have invited

13.

for	since
a month	I started school
a moment	the snow fell
2 weeks	my birthday
a long time	1987
over 3 years	winter
about 20 minutes	last autumn
a few years	midnight
three hours	he was a small boy
a whole day	the accident

14. a) playing tennis since
b) swimming for
c) have been cleaning, since
d) have been playing football for
e) have been talking, since
f) have been reading, for

15. was born, built, made, added, became, was, was born, For, have been enjoying, has become, have played, since, have been playing, have always gone, has always been, has only had, since, For, have been building

16. YOU: When were you born?
EXCHANGE: I was born on 26 March 1987 (in Newcastle-upon-Tyne).
YOU: How many brothers and sisters have you got?
EXCHANGE: I've got two: one sister and one brother.
YOU: When were they born?
EXCHANGE: My sister was born on 23 February 1989 and my brother was born on 19 February 1991.
YOU: How old were you when you started school?
EXCHANGE: I was five and a half. I started (school) in September 1992.
YOU: Have you ever learned a musical instrument?
EXCHANGE: Yes, I have – the guitar and the drums but I don't play the guitar anymore.
YOU: When did you stop?
EXCHANGE: I stopped in January 1998.
YOU: How long have you been playing the drums?
EXCHANGE: I started in February 1998.

YOU:	Have you ever gone on holiday to Germany?
EXCHANGE:	Yes, I have. We went to the Rhine in 1994.
YOU:	What sport do you like?
EXCHANGE:	Judo.
YOU:	Oh, how long have you been doing it?
EXCHANGE:	I've been doing it since 1994.
YOU:	When did you start secondary school?
EXCHANGE:	I started in September 1997.
YOU:	Do you go to any clubs at school?
EXCHANGE:	Yes, I'm a member of the school theatre group.
YOU:	How long have you been in the club?
EXCHANGE:	I've been in the club/a member since November 1997.
YOU:	Have you always lived in this house?
EXCHANGE:	No, I haven't.
YOU:	When did you move here?
EXCHANGE:	We moved here in May 1998 so we've been living here for about one and half years*.

*Standpunkt: September 1999

17. a) was shining
b) were you lying
c) was bleeding
d) was wearing
e) was speaking
f) was riding
g) were standing
h) were getting in

The hidden word is: sleeping

18. a) started, was eating, rang
b) burnt/burned, fell
c) rang, heard, were playing
d) opened, walked, were
e) was walking, slipped, broke
f) cleaned, cooked
g) walked, visited
h) was breaking, went, arrived, caught
i) were travelling, had, had to, didn't enjoy
j) were having, came, asked, said

19. was walking, suddenly saw, was looking, came out, was standing, asked, didn't know, was, followed, was talking, (was) showing, thought, decided, wanted, looked, said

20. a) had gone
b) had left
c) had already repaired
d) had passed
e) had never eaten
f) had given, had stolen
g) had already learned
h) had left

21. a) When Jerry got up at 11.45 a.m. his mother had already taken the breakfast things off the table.
Jerry got up after his mother had already taken the breakfast things off the table.

b) The teacher made Cameron stay longer at school because he hadn't done his French homework.
Because Cameron hadn't done his French homework, the teacher made him stay longer at school.

c) Laura's mother was very angry with her because she had left her new jacket on the train.
Because Laura had left her new jacket on the train, her mother was very angry with her.

d) When Lauren arrived at 9.30 p.m., the party had already started.
When Lauren arrived at the party (at 9.30 p.m.), it had already started.
The party had already started when Lauren arrived at 9.30 p.m.

e) Randall's nose bled badly after/because he had had a fight with the class bully, Roger.
After Randall had had a fight with the class bully, Roger, his nose bled badly.

22. a) After their parents had given them £10 each to spend, they left and took the bus to St. Peter Port.

b) After they had looked at the map, Lottie and Matt (they) decided to cycle to St. Andrew to look at the Little Chapel.

c) After they had cycled along the road through Torteval and the Forest, they took the main road towards St. Andrew.

d) After/When they had gone past the airport, they had to cycle for another 10 minutes before they finally arrived/and finally arrived at the Little Chapel.

e) When/After they had eaten an ice-cream, they agreed to go to the German Underground Military Hospital which is also in St. Andrew.

f) After they had turned right at the crossroads in St. Andrew, they took the road which went down towards Moulin Huet Bay in St. Martin because Lottie wanted to visit the Moulin Huet Pottery and buy some souvenirs/wanted to buy some souvenirs at the Moulin Huet Pottery.

g) After Lottie had bought 2 big cups and a small mouse at the pottery, they ate their sandwiches and swam at the rocky beach there.

h) After they had got back on their bikes, they cycled up the coast road right through the town centre of St. Peter Port until they got to Belle Greve Bay in St. Sampsons.

i) After they had turned left at Belle Greve Bay, they went towards Grande Havre Bay. They used the smaller roads because they were quicker.

j) After they had eaten another ice cream and (had) drunk some cold water, Matt took some photos of an interesting old French tower at Grande Havre Bay.

k) After they had cycled down to Vazon Bay, which is the sandiest beach in Guernsey and where it is fun to surf, they had a long swim because it was so hot.
After they had decided to go for a second swim because it was so hot, they cycled down to Vazon Bay, which is the sandiest beach in Guernsey and where it is fun to surf, and had a long swim/and swam for a long time.

l) After they had dried themselves and packed their rucksacks, they cycled back to their holiday home all along the coast road but their parent were not yet there.

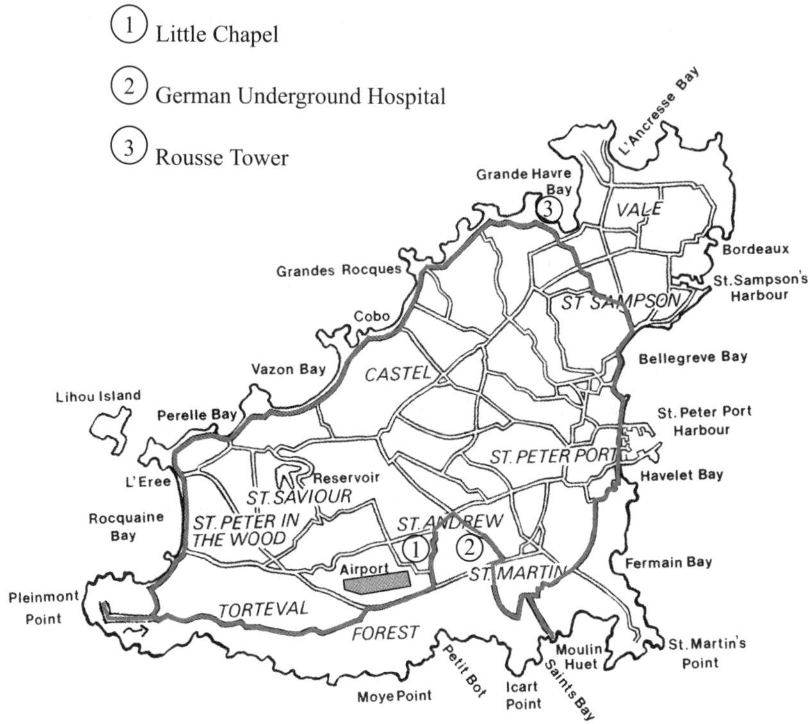
1 Little Chapel
2 German Underground Hospital
3 Rousse Tower
L'Ancresse Bay
Grande Havre Bay
VALE
Bordeaux
St. Sampson's Harbour
ST SAMPSON
Grandes Rocques
Cobo
Bellegreve Bay
Vazon Bay
CASTEL
Lihou Island
Perelle Bay
St. Peter Port Harbour
ST. PETER PORT
Havelet Bay
L'Eree
Reservoir
ST. SAVIOUR
Rocquaine Bay
ST. PETER IN THE WOOD
ST. ANDREW
Airport
ST. MARTIN
Fermain Bay
Pleinmont Point
TORTEVAL
FOREST
Petit Bot
Moulin Huet
Saints Bay
St. Martin's Point
Moye Point
Icart Point

Modale Hilfsverben

1. a) must/have to
b) had to
c) have to
d) have to
e) must
f) had to
g) has to
h) must/have to
i) had to
j) must

2. a) do you have to go?
b) do they have to do it in the evening?
c) did he have to see him?
d) will they have to do it?
e) many have you had to buy?
f) does she have to get up tomorrow?
g) has he had to help at home a lot this week?

3. a) don't have to (come with me)
b) didn't have to
c) doesn't have to
d) don't have to
e) won't have to do
f) don't have to

4. a) mustn't
b) mustn't
c) don't have to
d) don't have to
e) mustn't
f) mustn't
g) mustn't
h) don't have to
i) mustn't
j) don't have to
k) doesn't have to

5. You mustn't run in the corridor.
You must stand up and say "Good morning" or "Good afternoon" when a teacher comes into a classroom.

You are not allowed to leave the school during the week.
You must tidy up your room and change the sheets once a week.
You must turn the lights out at 8.30 p.m.
You aren't allowed to talk or listen to music when the lights are out.
You mustn't be rude to an older girl.

6. a) You mustn't drive on the right.
b) You needn't carry an ID card.
c) You must wear a school uniform.
d) You needn't get up so early for school.
e) You needn't say your surname when you answer the telephone.
f) You must go to school in the afternoon every day.
g) Most British policemen mustn't carry a gun.

7. a) When you're 16 you don't need to go to school any more.
b) In Britain many people think they don't need to clean their cars every Saturday. In Germany it's different!
c) Although the weather in Britain can be bad you needn't believe everything that you hear. It isn't always foggy and it doesn't always rain!
d) Visitors to Britain don't need to worry about the food: it's much better than most people say it is!
e) In Britain you needn't keep quiet on Sundays.

8. a) couldn't/wasn't able to
b) Can, can't
c) hasn't been able to
d) couldn't/wasn't able to
e) haven't been able to, can't
f) couldn't/wasn't able to
g) be able to, can, can't

9. a) could you
b) Can I
c) Can I
d) may/could I
e) Can/Could I

10. a) shall we
b) Shall I
c) will you
d) shall I
e) shall I
f) will you

11. a) Shall I take
b) Shall I close the window
c) shall I ring him up (and say sorry)
d) one shall I buy
e) Where shall we go out on Saturday?
f) Shall we go by tube
g) Shall we decorate the classroom (for his/Mr Linklater's birthday) or not?

12. a) ought to/should
b) oughtn't to/shouldn't
c) ought to/should
d) ought to/should
e) ought to/should
f) ought to/should

13. a) must
b) must
c) ought to/should
d) must
e) ought to/should
f) ought to/should

14. a) When you buy petrol you mustn't smoke.
b) Did you have to buy such a big dog?
c) Children under ten don't have to/needn't
d) Am I allowed to/May I/Could I go to bed a little later tonight?
e) In an exam you mustn't talk.
f) In most British schools children must wear a tie.
g) In some families boys needn't/don't need to help around the house at all.
h) Could I/Can I borrow £3 from you, mum, please till Saturday?

Passiv

1. a) Yesterday the pigs were fed at eight o'clock.
b) Yesterday the eggs were collected at half past eight.
c) Yesterday the cows were taken out into the field at nine o'clock.
d) Yesterday the tractor was repaired at ten o'clock.
e) Yesterday the barn was cleaned at half past eleven.
f) Yesterday the hay was made at three o'clock.
g) Yesterday the cows were brought in at six o'clock.
h) Yesterday the cows were milked at half past six.
i) Yesterday all the animals were fed at eight o'clock.

2. a) The fire-place in the living-room will have to be taken away.
b) The roof will have to be mended.
c) Some flowers will have to be planted.
d) The grass will have to be cut.
e) The fence will have to be painted.
f) The grass still hasn't been cut.
g) The door still hasn't been painted.
h) The windows still haven't been cleaned.
i) The rubbish still hasn't been taken away.

3. a) have to be worn
b) ought to/should be cleaned
c) must be/have to be fed
d) have to be worn
e) mustn't be taken

4.	a) 	a mechanic	repair	
	b) 	a chef	cook	
	c) 	a thief	steal	
	d) 	a doctor	do	
	e) 	a secretary	type	
	f) 	a teacher	correct	
	g) 	a nurse	take	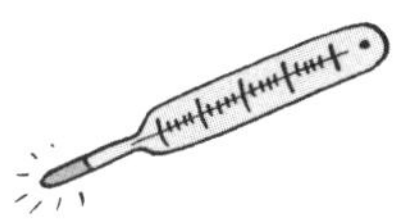
	h) 	a magician	do	
	i) 	a milkman	deliver	

a) Cars are repaired by a mechanic.
b) Meals are cooked by a chef.
c) Jewels are stolen by a thief.
d) Operations are done by a doctor.
e) Letters are typed by a secretary.
f) Homework is corrected by a teacher.
g) Temperatures are taken by a nurse.
h) Magic is done by a magician.
i) Milk is delivered by a milkman.

5. a) *We are the Champions* was sung by the band Queen.
b) *Robinson Crusoe* and *Moll Flanders* were written by Daniel Defoe.
c) The French and Napoleon were beaten at the battle of Waterloo by the Duke of Wellington.
d) The Conservative Party was led by Margaret Thatcher from 1975 to 1990/between 1975 and 1990.
e) Oxygen was discovered by Carl Wilhelm Scheele and Joseph Priestly in 1777.
f) The *Mona Lisa* was painted by Leonardo da Vinci.
g) London was destroyed by the Great Fire in 1666.
h) The atomic bomb was used against Japan by the United States for the first time on 6 August 1945.

6. was set up, was given, was done, were added, was made, were closed, (were) given, was started, were sent, was made, was taken off, were broken, (were) destroyed, were taken away, (were) used, was begun, was removed, was made, was planted, were done, was written, was bought

Gerundium

1. a) Playing chess is great.
b) Swimming is my favourite hobby.
c) Running is my best sport.
d) Climbing is dangerous.
e) Dancing is difficult.
f) Singing (in a choir at church) isn't stupid./isn't a stupid hobby.
g) Watching a lot of TV is boring.

2. a) No parking
b) No swimming
c) No taking photos

3. a) I love going out with my friends.
I love swimming.
b) I enjoy sewing my own clothes.
I enjoy doing maths.
c) I like mending things.
I like reading science fiction stories.
d) I don't like looking after my little brother
I don't like going on holiday with my family.
e) I hate helping in the garden.
I hate buying clothes.
f) I can't stand doing the washing up.
I can't stand tidying up my room.

4. a) He's good at taking photos.
b) He's good at speaking French.
c) She's good at playing badminton.
d) He's good at making /cooking pizza.

5.

gerund as subject	*gerund as object*	*gerund after adjective + preposition*
a) f)	c) d)	b) h)

The two 'trick' sentences are e and g.

6. a) Do you think collecting teddy-bears is an interesting hobby?

b) What was the name of that actor a long time ago who was also good at dancing?
≈ Do you mean Fred Astaire?
Yes, I do!

c) Why aren't you interested in coming with us?

d) I love shopping when I've got lots of money.

e) I think fishing is boring but a lot of people find it interesting.

f) Walking the dog is my job at home.

g) I hate watching horror films when I'm alone. And you?

Bedingungssätze

1. a) If the sun is hot, you will get brown.
b) If I save enough money, I'll buy myself the new Celine Dion CD.
c) If I leave now, I'll be able to catch the 10.48 train to Penzance.
d) If you lose your new jacket, I'll be very angry.
e) If you invite Rob to your party, I won't come.
f) If my mother loses her job, we won't be able to go on holiday this year.
g) If the factory closes, many people will be unemployed.
h) If it rains any more, the river will flood.
i) If the team wins today, we'll be first.
j) If it's a girl, we'll call it Emily.

2. If we send the Italians home, we won't have any pizza.
If we send the Indians home, we won't have any curry.
If we send the French home, we won't have much wine/cheese/many expensive clothes.
If we send the Japanese home, we won't have so many cameras/CD players/cars.
If we send the Chinese home, we won't have any Chinese restaurants/soya sauce.
If we send the Swiss home, we won't have any expensive watches/much chocolate/much cheese.
If we send the Germans home, we won't have any big cars/so many washing machines/hoovers/electrical things in the kitchen.

3. a) may/can
b) mustn't
c) must
d) may not
e) can/may
f) can't/may not
g) mustn't
h) can't

4. a) will/may/can
b) send, will/can get, do, won't/may not
c) won't start, don't leave

d) find, will tell
e) will have to, eat
f) buy, have
g) starts, will/can be
h) will be, put

5. a) would taste nice if it was less/wasn't so salty.
b) was less/wasn't so expensive/was cheaper, I would buy it.
c) was better/wasn't bad, I'd go on holiday in Britain.
d) would lend you some money if I had any.
e) didn't have to look after my little brother, I would go to the cinema with you.
f) was less/wasn't so cold/was warmer, we could have a barbecue.

6. a) If it snowed tomorrow, I'd be surprised.
b) If I won at Wimbledon this year, I'd be very happy.
c) If I change my hair colour, my mother may be angry.
d) If I did badly in the text next week, I'd be angry with myself.
e) If I had lots of money, I'd buy myself a new football.
f) If the sun shines tomorrow, we can go swimming.

7. Quiz

1. If my history teacher gave me two weeks to finish a project, I would think, "I won't be able to finish in time. Help!"
2. If my mother said I had got to tidy up my room before I was allowed to go shopping, I
   a) would push everything under the bed.
   b) wouldn't know where to start because it's so untidy.
   c) would start straight away and plan to do it properly. I'd be finished in about an hour or so.

3. If I wanted to get a part-time job so I could buy some new clothes, CDs, shoes, etc., I
   a) would dream all day about the 'perfect' job but wouldn't try to find one.
   b) would decide after half an hour that I didn't want to have a boss – or anybody else – who had to tell me what to do.
   c) would suddenly see that I was too busy to have a job.
4. If I promised my best friend to help get everything ready for his/her party, at 7 p.m. I
   a) would still be in my room because I couldn't decide what to wear.
   b) would be on the way to the house but I would be walking slowly because my friend always asks me to help and I have had enough.
   c) would still be in the supermarket because I couldn't decide what sort of food to buy.
5. If my friend asked me to go to the cinema with him (her) and the film started at 8 o'clock, I
   a) would arrive late but I would have a good excuse.
   b) might arrive late if I didn't think the film was very interesting.
   c) would arrive early and keep good seats for both of us.
6. If I wasn't interested in my boy/girlfriend much any more I
   a) would wait for him/her to say 'goodbye': somebody is/would be better than nobody. I would look for someone else at the same time.
   b) would several times 'forget' to meet him/her at our meeting place: I would hope he/she would/might soon understand why.
   c) would tell him/her straight away. I'm too honest and I think it is/I would think it was only fair to tell the truth.
7. If I got ketchup on my favourite pair of white trousers, I
   a) would wash the trousers straight away.
   b) would throw them in the back of the cupboard and only find them when was looking for a shoe.
   c) would hide them with the other washing and hope my mum didn't/wouldn't notice.
8. If my teacher gave me a test but I didn't understand the instructions, I
   a) would wait for someone else to ask.
   b) would say nothing because I wouldn't want anyone to think I was stupid.
   c) would say nothing because I would know the teacher had made the test extra hard and that she/he wouldn't help me anyway.

8. start, can drive, will need, want, wanted, could go, take, don't like, could visit, wanted, were interested, could go, like, we'll have to

9. a) When
b) If
c) when
d) when
e) If
f) If
g) when
h) If

10. a) Likely: If I buy some new shoes, they must be black.
Unlikely: If I bought some new shoes, they would have to be black.

b) Likely: If I go to a football match this week, I'll go with a friend.
Unlikely: If I went to a football match this week, I would go with a friend.

c) Likely: If I go to bed late this weekend, nobody will mind.
Unlikely: If I went to bed late this weekend, nobody would mind.

d) Likely: If I go to a party on Saturday, I'll have to wash my jeans.
Unlikely: If I went to a party on Saturday, I would have to wash my jeans.

e) Likely: If I have an English test soon, I'll do well.
Unlikely: If I had an English test soon, I'd do well.

f) Likely: If I find DM 50 in the road, I may keep it
Unlikely: If I found DM 50 in the road, I might keep it.

g) Likely: If I see a car accident, I'll ring the police.
Unlikely: If I saw a car accident, I'd ring the police.

h) Likely: If I get a summer job, I'll try and earn a lot of money.
Unlikely: If I got a summer job, I'd try and earn a lot of money.

i) Likely: If I write a letter to my grandmother, she'll be very happy.
Unlikely: If I wrote a letter to my grandmother, she'd be very happy.

Relativsätze

1. a) who/that
b) which/that
c) which/that
d) which/that
e) who/that
f) whose
g) who/that
h) which/that
i) whose
j) which/that

2. a) is a wild animal which looks like a dog.
b) is a piece of clothing which is worn over a shirt/which is made of wool/which means the same as jumper.
c) is a scientific subject which is taught at schools.
d) is someone/a person who writes books.
e) is a short letter which you send to a friend on holiday.
f) is a country which is part of Great Britain.
g) is someone/a person who comes from Asia.

3. a) My sister works for a company which makes films.
b) Have you ever met someone who can't speak English?
c) I don't know whose car the thieves stole.
d) I think it was George and Robert Stephenson who built the first steam train.
e) What was the name of the country which won the Football World Cup in 1998?
f) What's the name of the people who moved into that empty house last week?
g) What's the English word for someone who doesn't eat meat?
h) The Lake District is a National Park in Britain which attracts a lot of tourists in the summer.
i) Can you tell me the name of the London museum which is famous for its wax figures?
j) I bought some jeans yesterday which were not very expensive.
k) If you read a sign in a zoo which says "Don't feed the animals", you must follow the instructions.

4. a) Latin is a subject/language which is taught at/in some schools; is a language which was spoken long ago/a long time ago.

b) A lifeboat is a special boat which you use/need when an accident happens at sea.

c) A basket is something which you use to carry other things, for example when you go shopping.

d) Coal is something which you need to start a fire/which you find under the ground and which is black.

e) A sailor is a person/someone who works and lives on a boat.

f) A rabbit is an animal which has long ears/which has a short, white tail/which has big front teeth.

5. a) My neighbours have got a new dog whose name is Nellie.

b) I saw a good film on TV last night whose name I've already forgotten.

c) What's the name of the girl whose party you went to (at the weekend)?

d) Alan Shearer was a member of the English football team in 1998 whose main job was to score goals and to be captain.

e) I borrowed a book from the library this afternoon whose cover was already torn.

f) Leonardo di Caprio is a very famous actor whose face is loved by many girls.

6. a) Ludwig van Beethoven was a famous German composer who wrote the opera *Fidelio* and the symphony *Pastoral*.

b) John Adams was the man who was President of the United States of America after George Washington.

c) Prince Albert was the son of the Duke of Saxe-Coburg-Gotha who married Queen Victoria in 1840.

d) Sir Benjamin Baker was an/the English civil engineer who built the Forth Bridge in Scotland with Sir John Fowler and the London Metropolitan railway.

e) Robert Burns was a Scottish poet whose best-known poems are *Auld Lang Syne* and *The Banks of Doon*.

7.

religious knowledge	teaches us about our bodies, plants and animal life.
history	is all about numbers, fractions (¼ and ½), percentages (10 %) and shapes (▲ □ ○).
geography	talks about dates, wars and people who lived a long time ago.
biology	has to do with God and what people believe in other countries.
maths	is all about other countries and the weather there and the things these countries produce.

8. a) Geography is the subject which is all about countries and the weather there and the things these countries produce.

b) Religious knowledge is the subject which has to do with God and what people believe in other countries.

c) History is the subject which talks about dates, wars and people who lived a long time ago.

d) Biology is the subject which teaches us about our bodies, plants and animal life.

e) Maths is the subject which is all about numbers, fractions (¼ and ½), percentages (10 %) and shapes (▲ □ ○).

9. a) Have you found the door key you lost yesterday?

b) The shoes I bought last month have already got a hole in them.

c) The film we tried to go to yesterday was sold out.

d) I don't like the new pupil in our class.

e) The English family we met last year have invited us to visit them.

f) I would like to borrow the new CD Peter bought on Monday.

g) The new glasses Pat is wearing look nice.

h) The stories my uncle tells me are always funny.

10. which, which, who, (which), whose, whose, which, which, who, which, (which), (which), (which), which, which, who, (which), (which)

11. a) The flat which/that we live in is very noisy.
b) The holiday which/that my parents went on last month was terrible.
c) The small village which/that David's sister lives in is quite near Manchester.
d) The friend who/that I spent an hour in hospital with yesterday broke her leg in a bicycle accident.
e) The car which/that Julie ran into was not damaged badly.
f) The two friends who/that I painted my bedroom with are called Sam and Fiona.
g) The interesting castle which/that we went to in northern England is called Castle Howard.
h) The new bed which/that I slept in last night is very comfortable.

12. a) in which
b) to which
c) In which
d) on which
e) in which
f) from which
g) With which
h) at which
i) in which
j) In which, in which
k) At which

13. a) She lives in Buckingham Palace.
b) They go to Eton.
c) They stay in Scotland.
d) She was killed on 31st August 1997.
e) She was born in 1900.
f) He originally comes from Greece.
g) She spends a lot of time with dogs and horses.
h) He's very good at polo.
i) Prince Charles was born in 1948; Princess Anne was born in 1950; Prince Andrew was born in 1960 and Prince Edward was born in 1964.
j) She was buried in Althorpe in Northamptonshire.
k) They wear them at Ascot.

14. which, (which), who, who, whose, (which), which, to, which, (which), for, which

Ihre Meinung ist uns wichtig!

Ihre Anregungen sind uns immer willkommen. Bitte informieren Sie uns mit diesem Schein über Ihre Verbesserungsvorschläge!

Titel-Nr.	Seite	Vorschlag

Bitte hier abtrennen

Zutreffendes bitte ankreuzen!

Die Absenderin/der Absender ist:

- ☐ Lehrer/in in den Klassenstufen: ____
- ☐ Fachbetreuer/in
  Fächer: ____
- ☐ Seminarlehrer/in
  Fächer: ____
- ☐ Regierungsfachberater/in
  Fächer: ____
- ☐ Oberstufenbetreuer/in
- ☐ Schulleiter/in
- ☐ Referendar/in, Termin 2. Staatsexamen: ____
- ☐ Leiter/in Lehrerbibliothek
- ☐ Leiter/in Schülerbibliothek
- ☐ Sekretariat
- ☐ Eltern
- ☐ Schüler/in, Klasse: ____
- ☐ Sonstiges: ____

Unterrichtsfächer: **(Bei Lehrkräften!)**

____

STARK Verlag
Postfach 1852
85318 Freising

13-V1M

Bitte ausfüllen und im frankierten Umschlag an uns einsenden. Für Fensterkuverts geeignet.

Kennen Sie Ihre Kundennummer?
Bitte hier eintragen.

Absender **(Bitte in Druckbuchstaben!)**

Name/Vorname

Straße/Nr.

PLZ/Ort

Telefon privat

Geburtsjahr

E-Mail-Adresse

Schule/Schulstempel **(Bitte immer angeben!)**

(Bitte blättern Sie um)